THE MIRACLE
OF
SPONSORSHIP

Dear Deborah —
It was nice to
have lunch with
you. Love,
Karen Casey

A Hazelden Carry the Message Book

THE MIRACLE
OF
SPONSORSHIP

RECOVERY STORIES OF
HOPE AND RENEWAL

KAREN CASEY

HAZELDEN®

INFORMATION & EDUCATIONAL SERVICES

Hazelden
Center City, Minnesota 55012-0176

1-800-328-0094
1-651-213-4590 (Fax)
www.hazelden.org

Library of Congress Cataloging-in-Publication Data

Casey, Karen.
    The miracle of sponsorship : recovery stories of hope and renewal / Karen Casey.
        p. cm. — (A Hazelden carry the message book)
    ISBN 1-56838-553-6 (pbk.)
        1. Alcoholics—Rehabilitation. 2. Alcoholics Anonymous. 3. Sponsors. 4. Twelve-step
programs. I. Title. II. Series.

HV5275 .C37 2000
362.292'86—dc21
                                                                    00-044994

Author's note
The stories in this book are based on the lives of real people. Their names and specific circumstances have been changed to protect their anonymity.

Editor's note
The Twelve Steps are reprinted with permission of Alcoholics Anonymous World Services, Inc. (AAWS). Permission to reprint the Twelve Steps does not mean that AAWS has reviewed or approved the contents of this publication, or that AAWS necessarily agrees with the views expressed herein. AA is a program of recovery from alcoholism *only*—use of the Twelve Steps in connection with programs and activities which are patterned after AA, but which address other problems, or in any other non-AA context, does not imply otherwise.

04 03 02 01 00   6 5 4 3 2 1

Cover design by Adrian Morgan
Interior design by Elizabeth Cleveland
Typesetting by Stanton Publication Services, Inc.

DEDICATION

My life is a miracle that I can take very little credit for.
My friends and sponsors in Alcoholics Anonymous and
Al-Anon, along with my Higher Power and my husband,
Joe, deserve the credit for being my "way-showers." My
part was to show up and then keep showing up.

Thank God they all kept showing up, too!

CONTENTS

ACKNOWLEDGMENTS

First I want to acknowledge Rebecca Post, who explored with me the idea for this book while we sat in her office last summer. And then as my editor, she praised my efforts and encouraged my journey again and again. Linda Peterson comes to mind next. She has been a part of my writing life from the very beginning. *Each Day a New Beginning* passed through her hands nearly twenty years ago, and she has been rooting for me ever since. I can't thank her enough! I owe so much to the many people who so intimately shared their stories with me so that I could, in turn, share them with you here. They trusted me enough to hold nothing back. I love each of them, as you will when you hear their stories. Because of my desire to protect their anonymity, I have re-named them, but they will recognize themselves. Recovery is a partnership. None of us will make it without the helping hand of another person who cares. The stories here prove this. So does my life and yours, too.

Never stop offering your hand to the friends or strangers who appear on your path. It's not by accident that they are there.

INTRODUCTION

SPONSORSHIP: WHAT IT IS, HOW IT LOOKS, WHAT IT DOES

Sponsorship is a multidimensional aspect of my recovery. It can be the exchange of ideas between two individuals, one sharing with the other how he or she has handled an experience that mimics a situation that is troubling the listener. It might be a direct intervention of one person into the life of another when he or she is in serious trouble.

A sponsor often acts merely as the constant listener to the "sponsee" when she or he is struggling to determine the next, right thing to do in a situation. A sponsor, if relied on, prevents a recovering person from wallowing in isolation, the deadly condition that waits to ensnare any one of us if we get complacent about our individual healing and well-being. A sponsor may even appear to be the "accidental" listener when an altercation of some kind is occurring or when a person is about to make a disastrous decision but is caught, just in the nick of time.

Sponsorship need not be complicated, nor must it follow an explicit set of directions. Its primary purpose in every situation is to offer direction, solace, a presence; to nurture and acknowledge the holiness of the other; to foster healing in a person or a situation when disharmony threatens to destroy it. Sponsorship can happen any place, any time. It may not even be recognized as sponsorship at the time, but the healed or helped party will understand, in time, that something quite miraculous happened when the "sponsor" entered her life.

As must be apparent, I am defining sponsorship loosely, and that's intentional. While it is true that every one of us in the fellowship has come to rely on particular kinds of sponsors to help us handle particular kinds of problems, I don't want us to lose sight of the many other men and women who helped make our journey possible. Each of us has been ushered in a new direction, probably many times, on the journey to sobriety. I think it behooves us to honor all of those voices.

The idea for this book grew out of a discussion I had with two women who have been important in my life for many years. Both women had watched me change in many ways during the years of our friendship, and both were very much aware of my personal recovery from alcoholism. The topic of sponsorship arose, and I shared with them how dramatically my life changed as the result of a single person, a sponsor, so to speak, who intervened at just the right time many years ago, thus preventing my suicide. We talked further about how frequently an intervention such as this happens to people in all walks of life, and how very crucial such an intervention is in the lives of those who are trying to get sober and recover from an addiction. For us addicts, the slightest ripple in a life plan can throw us into a tailspin that only ends after relapse or worse has occurred. Were it not for the sponsorship role, so well and willingly played by hundreds of thousands of men and women, far fewer people would enjoy the fruits of a clean, sober, productive life. I can vouch for this. I am one of them.

ONE

A DIVINE PLAN AT WORK

MY STORY

I recently celebrated twenty-four years of continuous sobriety, and I am extremely happy and content with my life as a recovering woman, a wife, a writer, a sister, a daughter-in-law, an aunt, a grandmother, a mother-in-law, and a stepmother. I have traveled paths I would never have imagined for myself and have grown to expect a peacefulness that far surpasses anything I had dreamed of in my youth or, for that matter, even in my early and middle sobriety. But this would not be the case had I succeeded on a course I had charted for myself in the spring of 1977.

I went to my first Alcoholics Anonymous meeting in May 1976. The suggestion that I go was made by a counselor who was facilitating a couples group that I was attending alone because my significant other didn't choose to see "this group experience" as significant to our lives! The counselor dared to suggest that perhaps I needed to look at whether I was really in "a couple," and then went on to query me about my own alcohol and drug use. My answers, though reasonably honest, drew laughter from the group, and the counselor suggested

that perhaps AA was one of the solutions to my problem, not
only in this relationship but in other relationships, as well.

I figured I had nothing to lose by going and wanted to
please my counselor, so I agreed to meet two of the members
of my group at a designated time and place the following
Monday. My first AA experience was euphoric. I had never
seen so many good-looking men and women in one setting
for a long time. The smiles, the laughter, and the constant
hugging and introductions really took me by surprise. While
sitting in my first small group that night, I wasn't certain
whether I was really an alcoholic or not, but I knew I wanted
to be alcoholic! I wanted to feel and look like all of those
women, and I figured the way to do that was to mimic their
example.

I was also aware that the room was half-filled with attractive, successful-looking men, and it wasn't lost on me that
my counselor had already pointed out that I wasn't what she
would define as part of a couple. And that's who I was desperate to be. If John wasn't *the one*, then maybe one of these
men, present at this meeting, would fill the void. And wouldn't
you know, one of them approached me as the meeting was
ending and said, "Now be sure and come back next week!"
You can bet I did. I fantasized all week on how we (he and I)
would spend our future.

Fortunately for both of us, he had other plans and didn't
pursue me in spite of my overtures. Also fortunately for me,
two women, Kris and Eileen, became my constant companions. They convinced me that what I needed to learn was the
art of friendship with men and women. They set about showing me how to do this.

The first few months in recovery were as euphoric as the
first meeting had been. It was as though I had discovered a
new drug. I went to many meetings every week with many of

the same people I met at the first one in May. We socialized over dinner before the meetings and over dessert after the meetings. Every weekend was filled with activities for our sober crowd: parties, roller-skating, movies, more dinners, candlelight meetings, tennis, skiing and more. I had never had so many invitations to do so many different things in my entire life. I was ecstatic about how my life had changed and was convinced that every member of the entire human race would be happier if they had just such a program as AA in their lives. And all of this happiness had come to me simply because I had quit drinking and doing other drugs.

I can't say with certainty that I even comprehended the severity of my addiction in the early months. I just knew that I wanted to belong to this happy collection of individuals and that was enough for me. My part was to keep going wherever they were and learn by following their example. I was successful for some time. I was a good "student," so to speak, which wasn't unusual. At that time I was finishing a Ph.D. in American Studies at the University of Minnesota, and I surprised myself at how dedicated I was to being an A student there. I transferred that same talent to this new setting. For a time, it worked.

THE PINK CLOUD TEARS

But all was not well forever. The pink cloud I rested on began to tear and sport holes, and I started grabbing onto its edge for dear life. I can't recall any longer just exactly when my state of well-being began to change. I can only assure you it did. Did one thing trigger it? I don't think so, but the amorphous, insidious feelings of undefined, unspecified fear began to settle over me and invade every experience in my life. Not totally at first. The fear would come and go. Some mornings I would awaken, certain that I could go through the motions of my life, untroubled all day. But often, before the afternoon was over, I was terrified, and I didn't know what had triggered it. Program friends had a name for it: free-floating anxiety. Unfortunately, naming it didn't extinguish it.

Within weeks, I had succumbed to near isolation. I sat up many nights, longing for the solace I used to get from sipping alcohol into the wee hours. I avoided meetings; I didn't want anyone to know what a basket case I had become. I seldom called sponsors or friends on the phone. I had an image to protect. After all, I was getting a Ph.D. If others saw me like this, what then? I soon became afraid to appear before my night school students, too, certain they would grill me on information I no longer had command of. Thus, I repeatedly didn't report to class and left the college and the students wondering.

As the weeks passed and the anxiety remained, I began to dream of suicide. It was a familiar dream, one I had had many times before getting sober. Its contemplation had always been my "out," the refuge for my troubled soul. I had first shared this admission with a psychiatrist many years earlier, long before I ended up in AA. I had always seen suicide as a solution, a sensible one, in fact, if life's circumstances became more than I could handle. This dream had come to me even as a teenager. The doctor was quick to tell me that suicide was never seen as an option by mentally healthy people. I can still remember how I doubted her words. I was certain she was wrong. I didn't feel mentally sick. I didn't fit any image I had of the mentally ill at that time.

I still don't think I was mentally ill. I was just scared and desperate and so certain that my feelings would never change. Not being courageous enough to show up for classes or meetings or events of any kind made my existence superfluous at the very least. I sat in my small, one-bedroom apartment and counted the windows and the towels I would need for stuffing around their openings. I checked to make sure that I had matches for lighting the gas stove. I had quit smoking a few months earlier, so matches were not always available. Suicide seemed so simple. I would have no more fear. Nor would I need to plan my avoidance of people and places I couldn't face. All I had to do was pick up the towels and begin the task of placing them on the sills, as close as possible to the window openings. And then I heard a knock at the door.

A FORGOTTEN APPOINTMENT

I hesitated for a moment but the knocking continued, so I walked over to the door and softly asked, "Who is there?" A voice responded, "Pat." I could think of no friend named Pat. I was silent for a time and she said, quite authoritatively, "We have an appointment, Karen. Don't you remember?" Reluctantly, I opened the door, and she came in, brushing past me. She looked familiar enough, but I was still uncertain as to why she was here. She obviously could see the puzzlement on my face and said, "Don't you remember? We made an appointment to discuss your financial plan while drinking coffee at Unity Church a few weeks back. I am a financial planner." Although I said of course I remember, I didn't. I earned very little as an instructor at the University of Minnesota at the time and had no need of a financial planner. But she insisted that we had made the appointment, showing me her appointment book in case I still doubted her, so I asked her to sit down at the kitchen table.

Her next question surprised me. "What's the matter?" I stammered at first and then told her I was extremely depressed. She asked me if I knew why. I said that I was a recovering alcoholic and was feeling overwhelmed by free-floating anxiety. I described how dramatically my life had changed over the last few weeks, how I had gone from near constant euphoria to the dread of waking up in the morning. How I was no longer comfortable at meetings, talking to friends, and worst of all, appearing before my students at the university. I admitted that I had considered suicide, but I wasn't forthcoming with how detailed my plans actually were. She never asked about the towels stacked on my kitchen table. She probably thought I had just finished a load of wash.

Her next comment took me completely by surprise. She said she was envious of me! For a moment all I could think of was what a crazy woman she must be, but she quickly went on to explain her comment. She said what I was experiencing was a spiritual process that she called "chemicalization." She said she first learned about this process in a book by Katherine Ponder titled *The Dynamic Laws of Healing.* She explained Ponder's message in this way: when a person is moving to a new spiritual plane of understanding, the old, formerly entrenched ideas spring into action in a last ditch attempt to prevent new ideas from claiming hold on the mind. The struggle that ensues pushes the psyche to an extreme level of agitation and uncertainty. Thus the feeling of free-floating anxiety is given a resting place. Pat assured me that I was exactly where I needed to be and that these feelings of overwhelming fear would leave just as mysteriously as they came if I trusted that God was part of the process.

Quite suddenly, my mood began to change. For the first time in many weeks, I felt a tiny glimmer of hope and relief. This woman, who had come to talk to me about financial planning, had offered me something that all the money in the world couldn't have offered me. She offered me a fresh understanding of my unsettled condition, and peace began to seep into my consciousness. After a few more minutes, we concluded that our visit was at an end. My financial condition wasn't ever mentioned. Pat got up, gave me a warm hug, and I walked her to the door. After she left, I sat down on the couch and knew that I would be okay. I knew that God was close at hand. I knew that God had, in fact, sent Pat to me in a prearranged way: the appointment I had made with her some weeks before, an appointment that I never remembered having made.

WE ARE NEVER ALONE

This experience assured me then and does to this day that whatever one is experiencing, it doesn't have to be shouldered alone. We are never alone, never ever. A divine plan is always at work. I also became convinced from that day forward that whoever comes into our lives has a message for us. We may not at first appreciate the message. We may not even want to listen to it, but if we can overcome our resistance, as I did with Pat, our experiences can dramatically change. Nothing is ever coincidental. Our willingness to learn is all that we need to offer any time, to any situation, or to any person.

Pat wasn't my official sponsor in AA, but she was God's sponsor. That is a fact that I never doubted from the moment she spoke so understandingly of the turmoil I had been undergoing for many weeks. From that day forward, I realized that sponsors can enter our lives at any time, in any disguise, with myriad messages. But their one constant is their offering of hope, a changed perspective, on whatever condition has us troubled at the moment. Pat quite literally saved my life on that spring day in 1977. Since that time, I have gone on to be productive in many ways. Were it not for Pat, I would never have written *Each Day a New Beginning* or the eleven other books that followed the first one. I know she was my guardian angel. And as certain as I am of that, I am certain that you, too, have a guardian angel looking over your shoulder. You may not recognize him or her, but your angel is there with messages for you. I hope you are as intent on listening as I have become.

So you can see that sponsors may appear to us in many ways. The ones we choose in AA or other Twelve Step programs to gather the specific information we need about how to work the Steps, how to avoid the pitfalls, and how to "read" the experiences we find ourselves confronting on a daily basis must be honored, but these sponsors aren't the only individuals that God may use to help us fulfill the plans necessary for the unfolding of our lives. Actually, it is quite possible that God will send someone our way that we'd never, in a thousand years, imagine was in our life purposefully.

In the stories that follow, you will see many times how varied the role of sponsorship actually is, how it can change instantly, how it unfolds, sometimes loudly and sometimes very quietly, and what it can do for a person, for his or her family, and finally for the whole human race. What touches one of us, in time, touches all of us. That's the miracle of one person helping another.

GOD-INSPIRED INTERVENTIONS

The stories that follow in this book reflect a format familiar to us in AA. As you read the stories, you will discover "what it was like, what happened, and what it's like now" for those who talked to me about the role of sponsorship in their lives.

We are so blessed to be walking this path together. Not one of us would be here now if it weren't for the recovery program given birth by Bill W. and Dr. Bob. Every individual whom each one of us encounters on a daily basis is being affected by the legacy these two men left behind. Were it not for their teachings and, even more important, our willingness to put into practice their suggestions, the lives we lead and the lives of those around us would be far different.

Our recovery from addiction is the direct result of Bill and Bob's willingness to listen to the various people who intervened in their lives. That's what this book is about: interventions, interventions that were God inspired.

Seldom do we realize the profound meaning of a particular instant or set of circumstances. Hindsight always enlightens us, however. That's how it was for all of the people who gladly shared their experiences, strength, and hope with me. At first they didn't understand the significance of a certain interaction with a particular individual, and only later came to see it as a turning point. That they wanted to share with you what they had gained from their experiences is what makes this program work for them, for us, and for all of the people who will follow us. We have been told from the very first that we must "give it away in order to keep it." With that thought in mind, read on.

TWO

WE'RE NEVER TOO SICK
TO GET BETTER

REBA'S STORY

Reba came into my life in a significant way little more than two years ago. I had been seeing her in a gym where I worked out on a regular basis, and something about her attracted my attention. She always seemed to have a smile for everyone, a quiet "hello, how are you," but she was also very intent on her workout program.

Unlike many who wander into a gym, she was there with a purpose, not to socialize and kill time until her next daily appointment. And her physical condition revealed it. She was fit in every way. She was strong. As she moved from one machine to the next, she concentrated on the effects she was seeking for her body, effects she had succeeded in accomplishing, I noted. She had not an ounce of body fat. She was lean, long-legged, and very tan.

I saw her outside of the gym for the first time when I wandered into a health food store and restaurant. She worked there as the clinical nutritionist. Now her physical appearance made even more sense to me. Not only was she serious about how she exercised and conditioned her body, but she was serious about what she put in it. For the first time, we spoke briefly, commenting on our "shared interests" of good nutrition and healthy fitness. What I didn't know then was that we also shared the program of recovery.

That piece of information emerged some weeks later when we rode exercise bikes side by side. We talked about our lives more personally: where we were born, where we lived, what brought us to Florida; about husbands, children, educational backgrounds, professions. And then we broached the topic of spirituality. I can no longer recall exactly what triggered my self-disclosure, but I revealed that I was a "Twelve Stepper." Any of you reading this knows how uplifting it is when you dare to share this kind of information and the listener says, "Me, too." From that moment on, Reba and I gave a few special minutes to each other whenever we happened to be in the gym at the same time. Just knowing we shared this special path meant we could converse even though silent on many of our trips to the gym. A smile was all that was necessary for us to know we were willing to help each other if the need ever arose.

Over the next few months, our friendship flourished. I shared with her many bits and pieces of my journey, and she did likewise. We discovered, in the process of our sharing, that she had been reading a couple of my earlier books for a period of many years. This surprised and tickled both of us. Who would ever have thought this possible? Certainly not me. Before my scheduled return to Minnesota for the summer months, we began contemplating how we might find the time to get to know each other better. Reba suggested a trip together. Neither of us had spent any time in the Southwest, so the destination appealed to both of us. Before long our plans were made. I returned to Minnesota for the summer, and we stayed in contact by phone or by e-mail until we met at the airport in Arizona.

THE ROLLER COASTER OF ADDICTION

It was on that trip that Reba shared with me the story I am about to share with you. It had not been our intent to talk so seriously on this trip. I had not gone west seeking the story she shared, but I was deeply moved by it and knew it was a story I wanted to share with others. Reba's story, though different from my story and no doubt from yours, contains the element of intervention by "sponsors" sent by God. As with so many of us, too, they generally came just in the nick of time.

Reba's addiction was triggered in her early teens. Affluence and extremely well-educated parents didn't protect her or steer her away from taking a path so common to many of us. First alcohol, then drugs, and finally an addictive relationship with food claimed her every waking moment. Under the guise of being an exceptional student (which she was), she managed to avoid the constant purview of her family, particularly her mother, a practicing psychologist. By entering college and moving out on her own when she was only seventeen years old, she "escaped." Her escape was successful for a time. She succeeded as a student and as a drug addict. Her family was never far away, however. She saw them frequently. But when she needed to perform for a family event, she was able to. In fact, she was very good at it. She was on stage. Not even her mother, who worked with addicts much of the time, could guess the events that really made up Reba's life away from home.

The roller coaster of addiction was Reba's trip for many years. She excelled in college in spite of her addictions, a feat many of us have managed. After college, Reba married her first husband, and they had two boys. She was still very much the addict, but she was also very capable, able to handle her many tasks as mother, wife, and employee. Perhaps it was fortunate that Reba's husband was an alcoholic, too, because it was through the suggestion of a loving friend, one of those instances we can label God-inspired, that she eventually sought the help of Al-Anon to live with his addiction. After just one meeting, she felt for the first time that she had found "a family" who understood at least part of her life. The welcoming hugs ushered in a sense of hope for her life that she had never experienced before. Her family's wealth, prestige, and education had never been able to offer her the security and comfort she now found in "these rooms."

She continued going to Al-Anon, and over time even began to suspect that some of her own behavior and use of chemicals resembled the characteristics of addiction. However, acceptance of her own alcoholism and drug addiction was not yet even imaginable.

Although Reba's first marriage didn't survive, some might say fortunately, its importance to her evolution was profound, because her involvement with a Twelve Step fellowship did survive. She joined Alcoholics Anonymous, not long after her husband left, during therapy with her son, and that's one of the miracles of her story. Why didn't she walk away from our program of recovery when her husband walked away from her and their two children? What kept her intrigued and "coming back"?

Reba's boys, though a blessing, came with lessons galore for all the people who shared their paths. Prior to Reba's complete freedom from her own drug use, she was, as a single parent, in therapy with one of her sons. By this time she was no longer supported financially by the boys' father. He had not been present in their lives for some time. Therapy was triggered by her son Toby's extremely cruel and dangerous behaviors, actions that Reba could neither understand nor tolerate. She kept asking herself, Is my son simply evil? Am I just a bad parent? Or is there help for him and me and my other son, too?

A CIRCUITOUS ROUTE

The help that eventually arrived was extremely significant. Among other things, the therapist insisted that Reba remain drug- and alcohol-free while in therapy with Toby. Thus his therapy resulted in Reba totally relinquishing her use of alcohol and other drugs, a relationship that had taken root in her youth and that was painstakingly nurtured in her twenties and thirties. She wasn't happy about giving up her dependence on alcohol and drugs; they had offered her the only solace she had had for many years, but the severity of her son's condition made any other choice impossible. The therapist, and in a circuitous way her son, too, served as the catalysts, "the sponsors," who pointed out to Reba the road to follow, a path that ultimately led her to a far different kind of life, and in time, a very different spiritual understanding of her life.

By the time of Toby's involvement in therapy, drugs weren't the only substances over which Reba had lost control. Her relationship with food had also become addictive. However, dealing with that issue wasn't on the agenda for the time being. In fact, bingeing and purging were behaviors she kept hidden from all eyes. She tried to ignore them as well, because even she didn't understand them. She definitely wasn't interested in sharing them with her son's therapist. It seemed necessary to her to focus on first things first, and her son was first.

At the unexpected suggestion of Toby's therapist, Reba agreed to go to AA. The miracle is that although she was surprised, she wasn't mad or threatened by the suggestion and was able to go with an open heart and mind. Eventually she developed a "little willingness" to trust what others were saying. She had never allowed herself to trust her family of origin. Nor had she developed any trust of her husband in her first marriage. Not one therapist (and there had been many) and not a single family member had received anything like the reverence that she so surprisingly, and willingly and promptly, offered to her new friends in the fellowship of Alcoholics Anonymous. While in therapy, Reba clung to the messages of these new friends and carried home their hope until she was able to create the feeling of hope herself. But the real turning point for Reba in AA was her relationship with her first sponsor.

NO EASIER, SOFTER WAY

Marge was a no-nonsense sort of woman who had been sober for many years. She demanded that Reba do her AA work as instructed. If Reba questioned Marge's methods or if she tried to explain away her behaviors, "she could just get another sponsor. Period!" Reba assured me that this tough approach, though disarming and certainly not required or even suggested as the right way to sponsor in any of AA's published literature, was what she needed. Her family of origin had tried to ignore or explain away the obvious rather than deal with the ugliness. Reba had always done it this way, too. She was beginning to realize her journey had to change. She wasn't certain how she knew this, she simply did; the tougher her sponsor, the better Reba responded. Marge's demands gave her an absolute path to walk, and Reba feared the easier, softer way.

She learned to say, and seriously mean, "Thank you for telling me that." And Marge assured Reba that she had nothing to lose from telling her the blunt truth. Reba said she really didn't understand most of what Marge was telling her initially, but she listened anyway and never dared to argue. She knew she wanted what others had, and the only way she could get it was by following their example and Marge's instructions. Marge insisted that every answer to every problem was in *Alcoholics Anonymous,* the Big Book of AA, and Reba was instructed to find those answers and utilize them if she wanted to survive. Hence, she read the Big Book, again and again, to make sure no answer was eluding her.

Thanks to Reba's desire to change, her hard work, and the intervention of her sponsor, she managed to stay clean and sober, but many details in her life were still chaotic. Raising two sometimes deeply troubled boys wasn't an easy job. Fortunately, her own career at a university served her well and gave her a sense of accomplishment. It ultimately also helped her address the other major addiction in her life: food. Even though Reba was clean and sober, her serenity was fleeting at best, because she had yet to confront her compulsion to binge and purge, a compulsion that had ruled her life for years.

Do you suppose Reba's master's degree in nutrition was coincidental? Hardly. We have all learned, with the help of others in this program, that there are no coincidences. *God is always doing for us what we have been unable to do for ourselves.* And until Reba was ready to acknowledge and address this addiction in her life, God was merely nudging her along the path to do some of the work that would prepare her, not only for helping herself, but for helping thousands of others, too. The good news is that sometimes we simply can't ignore the signs anymore; we can't pretend, in good conscience, not to notice where we seem to be going in spite of ourselves. This awareness, coupled with the damaging effects of bingeing and purging on Reba's body, moved her, at last, in yet another direction.

A HEAP OF TROUBLES

Before Reba's life turned around, however, there was a brief second marriage and a second divorce, and chaos still reigned in her small family. Eventually she wandered into a third marriage, to a man who shared the program of recovery, surely a departure from the experiences she had lived through in the other two marriages. At least in this union, she felt certain there would be no more guns held to her head, no more fear for her own life or fear for the lives of her boys. Reba was certain that "sharing the principles of this program" with a life partner would ensure the serenity she craved so much. But it was soon apparent that all was not well in this marriage, either.

To make a life with her new husband, Reba had to move to another state, which also meant leaving her solid support system behind. Even more difficult than dealing with this aspect of the marriage, her relocation also meant leaving one son behind, the son who had been so troubled. Not easy decisions for Reba, but necessary for a woman who still believed in the possibility of peace and hope and love. Her younger son, Mike, simply couldn't survive the torment experienced at the hands of Toby, so Reba sought the help of her mother, who professionally counseled troubled families every day. She agreed to take Toby in, and the newly married couple and Mike moved and started life anew. Mike and Reba's husband struggled to forge a relationship that met both their needs, but they had not yet succeeded at the time that Reba and I talked. She was struggling to let them have whatever relationship they each needed while she struggled to find relief from her compulsion to binge and purge.

It often seems that when a person has had enough to cope with, too much in fact, even more gets heaped on her. Toby, while living with Reba's mother, was doing better, but Mike, her younger son, was sad and lonely and unable to relate to his "new dad." And husband number three was far from being the loving individual, "the savior," Reba had believed him to be. His own recovery from drug and alcohol addiction needed work, as did hers, and they were unable to be for each other what they each sought.

Fortunately for Reba, a different kind of sponsor came into her life at this time. Marge, her tough first sponsor, had been the right sponsor for Reba's introduction to this life pathway because Reba had been able to evade the prying eyes of others so successfully most of her life. But what she needed now was a gentle, compassionate approach, a sponsor who would promise that things could get better as long as Reba kept listening and praying and talking to the other recovering people around her. She needed no more reprimands. Now she needed the courage to believe that wherever she was, she was meant to be. And she found that kind of woman in Lois. Lois was always there to listen and encourage, and she convinced Reba that her path was "inspired." This brought great relief to Reba, who had seldom experienced the inner assurance that "all was well." In particular, Lois taught Reba that though she was still relatively new in recovery, she had already learned enough to be giving back to others. This was a real turning point for Reba.

Reba's role as a sponsor began to take form. Like Marge, her first sponsor, Reba was tough and demanded that sponsees follow *the book*. Her job was to pass on the AA program,

not push or even suggest related books and ideas to her sponsees. There was one way to get and stay sober. That was what
she had learned from Marge and what she now taught.

Sponsorship, though an important dimension to her life,
didn't solve the problems Reba still confronted at home.
Where were those solutions to come from? Fortunately she
still hoped there were benefits to therapy. That, coupled with
the many meetings she attended, would surely light her way.
But the going was rough, and her steps remained uncertain.
The haunting question was, "Why don't the others in my life
change as I have changed?"

It was during this period of time that Reba entered my
life. I had missed out on her active addictions, her earlier
marriages, and the presence of Toby, her oldest son. I got to
know the woman who was committed to the sober, abstinent
life, the life that included meetings, work, fitness, a sensible
eating program, and frolic in the sun. But I also got to know
the woman who still longed for the serenity and the love she
felt she had been promised by this program and in this marriage, but which still eluded her. I had no answers except
what had worked for me.

A MESSAGE IN THE MADNESS

I wasn't asked to be her sponsor, but as I said earlier in this
book, the introduction of someone new in one's life can
often be considered God's way of making sure that at least
one of us gets his message. My message to her, because of
what it had done for me, was "go to Al-Anon" again. I don't
want to imply, in any way, that I was a significant "intervener"
in her life, but I have learned and I do believe that God always
brings us together with those individuals who have a particular message for us. And equally important, in my view, is that

whatever message any one of us is inspired to give is one we must need to hear once again, as well. I do not doubt my need for Al-Anon, and I will be as committed to it as I am to my AA program for as long as I live. Having an opportunity to share what the Al-Anon program had done and was continuing to do for my life was valuable, perhaps to both of us. It is the message of hope I offered to her when we talked.

Reba's struggles are not over, as of the writing of this book, but she has committed herself once again to the principles of Al-Anon, along with the principles of AA and Overeaters Anonymous, as the pathway to the life she deserves and prays for. From each therapist and every sponsor and friend she has turned to, she has received the messages she needed, messages that encouraged her to keep moving forward, and as a result, she has maintained her abstinence from all harmful chemicals for all the years of her involvement with this program.

Not all interventions are as overtly dramatic as the time when Pat knocked on my apartment door, literally saving me from a carefully planned suicide. But each intervention, in its own way, is saving a person from harm of some kind. And harm of any kind, when not avoided, can lead to places far too dark for a return trip to be possible. We have all known an individual or two who has escaped down one of those dark paths, never to return. And although Reba's first sponsor told her, "Some of us have to die in order for others to live," none of us wants to stand by while that happens. Each of us hopes that God will call one of us to do his work in the nick of time.

SPONSORS WEAR MANY FACES

A sponsor doesn't need to be previously involved with your life, not even on a casual basis. He or she may have simply

stood next to you in line at the grocery. Recall how far removed Pat was from my life, yet she appeared at my door at
just the right moment. A sponsor doesn't need to be a member of a Twelve Step program. Reba's therapists were not all
Twelve Step members. But they did point her in a direction
that was right for her, where real help was available, and
that's the key element. A sponsor, as I am using the term in
this book, doesn't have to understand your specific life, your
specific addiction, or your specific struggle. He or she
doesn't need to know how seriously dangerous your current
condition might be. In fact, your sponsor might never know
that what he or she said to you made a difference in how your
life unfolded from that moment on. It's even quite possible
that you won't recognize their words as life-saving instructions at the time they are voiced.

But sponsorship, in its purest sense, is about sharing ideas
that make sense to ears that are willing to listen. It's not a
complicated relationship. It's little more than one heart trying to touch another heart, on behalf of all of our hearts. Put
this way, however, we might agree that it's not little at all but
terribly big and massively profound. It's a source of joy to be
a part of this wonderful aspect of God's plans.

Reba's story reiterates some aspects of sponsorship. Marge
became a very present influence on how Reba observed her
actions. She taught Reba to rely on the suggestions of others
who had walked in her shoes, and she showed Reba that life
could be lived free from constant fear. Teaching by example
was easy for Marge, and Reba was a good student. She showed
Reba what unconditional love really meant. She was tough,
but she didn't judge Reba in harmful ways. Reba very soon
learned that she could share all of herself with Marge, certainly things she had never dared to reveal to her mom or dad
or siblings.

Reba learned about honesty and self-respect and hard work from Marge, and she learned about honoring our softer side and offering love to others from Lois. From both she learned that we are never too sick to get better, nor are we ever too "well" to no longer need constant, vigilant, and objective input from the men and women who share our journey. She learned to celebrate the reality that, as recovering people, we are in process. We are not finished products. That makes the adventure that lies before us worth arising for each day.

THREE

WHEREVER WE ARE IS
WHERE WE ARE NEEDED

MATT'S STORY

Matt has enjoyed more than twenty years of continuous abstinence from alcohol and other drugs. He didn't come easily to
this program we share, however. He was definitely not glad
about needing it. He had watched others in his family need
the program, and he was certainly not planning to succumb.

Matt had enjoyed the fruits of his work for many years, un-
encumbered by a wife or kids. He hadn't planned to include
such trappings in his life. To be free to move, to travel, to answer to no one, in fact to escape everyone, intrigued him far
more than the idea of a family. His own family of origin had
been chaotic at best and insane at worst. They numbered ten.
Dad was a hardworking, breadwinning, Irish Catholic, and
mostly absent alcoholic. Mom was the perfect martyr, always
trying to pretend that nothing was wrong while trying to
manage the escapades of eight out-of-control children. Matt,
the only boy and the second oldest child, managed to escape
Mom's purview much of the time, but not Dad's.

With him, Matt trudged to the neighborhood bar on too

many occasions, only to be laughed at by the other patrons because his ears stuck out and his pants were too short. Dad had a specific way of lifting Matt up by his ears and setting him on the bar to show his friends how really strong Matt's ears were. Matt's tears were ignored by his Dad's rheumy-eyed friends.

Matt learned to hide out as much as possible as soon as he was old enough to understand how his absence could save him from embarrassment and worse. He withdrew to his bedroom and into his imagination. He became good at drawing and building little cars, planes, birdhouses, and boxes with secret compartments. In fact, he could look at a picture in a book, draw it almost perfectly and then build it from scraps of wood and glue. He managed to entertain himself for hours at a time, thus saving himself from the embarrassment or chaos that reigned whenever the family was gathered together.

In junior high school he discovered girls, cigarettes, and cough syrup laced with alcohol. The mixture of all three made him feel like he was "the man!" What he failed to see then but was finally willing to acknowledge years later was that the chaos he'd grown up with he quite naturally carried into every relationship he had. And he hid out from each of those relationships, too, whenever the woman began to get too close.

For many years, he was undeterred by the turmoil that followed him wherever he went. He was simply intent on drinking, partying, and loving and leaving as many women as possible, but the interactions with one woman in particular, more intense interactions than with most of the others, would surface in a most unexpected way years later.

A GRADUAL SHIFT

Neither the Navy, which Matt joined at age seventeen upon high school graduation, nor innumerable geographic moves curbed his appetite or changed the outcomes of his relationships. The scenarios were always similar. As someone got close, it was time to move on. Needless to say, there were many moves. Finally, Matt returned to his hometown only to discover that Dad had tried to get sober, though not successfully, and two sisters had succeeded in getting sober, though not before one was judged to be insane and locked up for the better part of a year.

The entire family was still in turmoil, but their interactions were beginning to change. Those first in the program and those in therapy were quick to blame the parents as the root of all the problems. It would be many years, many "sponsors," and the passing of many events before the wisdom finally sank in that no single person is ever to blame for the evolution of a family, that each member has chosen a particular path for his or her own sought-after edification.

Matt came home to confusion and blame and fear about his future. His profession was intact, but direction in life was missing. His connections to others were superficial and fleeting, at best. And he began to fear waking up most days. The consumption of alcohol and drugs, though constants in his life, failed to relieve his ennui. The contemplation of suicide as the solution to his terror and loneliness was frequently recurring.

Then one sober sister dropped by unexpectedly for a visit. She walked in while Matt was toying with a pistol. He didn't reveal his thoughts. She didn't ask. But she did pick up the pistol and aim it at the target Matt had hanging at the end of the hallway to his garage. From the kitchen you could just barely make out the bull's-eye. She took careful aim and pulled the trigger. Zing! She hit the bull's-eye. Zing! Zing! Zing! She hit it three more times. Ten times in a row she hit the bull's-eye, to Matt's amazement. He asked her how she did it. She said that ever since she got sober life was easier. She could see with greater clarity.

She was gentle, not wild in her actions or her conversation, as so many times in their past, and she was still very funny. Her sense of humor was very much intact. He told her she seemed different, and he was intrigued with the difference even though he didn't understand it. He did know that if the difference was due to her being sober, he was not interested in following her path. Not yet, at least. However, her presence in his kitchen on that particular occasion was never far from his mind. The pain in his life continued. The suicide thoughts continued. The terror and loneliness continued. It wasn't too many months before he placed a call to her apartment. She said, "The time must be right. Come on over."

He listened intently to her story, her hope, and her suggestions for how he might find what she had found. He had decided he was willing to go at least part of the way for a different kind of life. And he did. For many years, up to a point, he walked the walk and talked the talk, but never wholeheartedly. He stayed sober but he didn't enjoy peace or serenity. He wasn't particularly bothered by their absence, either. He remained cynical and angry, and very funny as a way to cover up those attitudes, but not always successfully. He had developed a relationship with a woman who was also in recovery, and they managed to make their relationship work, but it wasn't a very peaceful partnership. Matt seldom sought the guidance of a sponsor, and he went to one weekly meeting, certainly not often enough to hear all of the messages that might have helped him.

A NEW CONNECTION TO PEOPLE

His wife had her own program, and the journey was rough for the two of them. Matt wasn't necessarily happy or unhappy. He went about his daily activities much as he had done as a child, often hiding out in his shop or in front of the television. He interacted with his wife or with friends when he needed to, but he was most content in the creative act of building something. And he built beautiful things: tables, and desks and chairs and cabins. He even built cars and canoes. His good feelings came from the praise he got for his creations, rather than from interactions with the significant people in his life. It wasn't that he didn't like people. He did, definitely. But he still struggled with letting them get close. Feeling separate was far more familiar.

And then some major shifts began to happen. First his dad died and his family grew closer. Then because of a suggestion made by a friend, he decided to explore another dimension to his spiritual program and became a student of *A Course in Miracles.* This exploration allowed him to appreciate a different kind of connection to people; in fact, it taught him that there is nothing but connection to others in this experience called life. The feelings of separation he had been haunted by his whole life began to recede, and he felt energized by the knowledge. His friend, the "sponsor" for this significant addition to his life, is someone he repeatedly acknowledges. His life has changed dramatically because of the few words she shared about her experiences, which were then coupled with his willingness to listen and become open to a new way to see his life.

But his story gets even more dramatic. One year around Christmastime, he got a letter from his former girlfriend saying their son had tracked her down. Did he want to be identified as the father? His first thought was fear. And then questions flooded his mind: "What does this mean? How would this fit into my life now? What about my wife?" He quickly sought out a friend and talked it over. His friend advised him to get a lawyer, quickly, believing that something bad could come of this. "What if the kid wants money or something?" the friend asked. Fortunately he made another call to his sponsor, Tom. Tom said, "Matt, it's a miracle! But go slow. Let the relationship develop naturally."

After discussing the girlfriend's letter and the comments by his friend and his sponsor with his wife, who agreed it was indeed a miracle, Matt called his son, and a new relationship began. Had Matt not made the second call, the one to his sponsor, he would have missed out on one of the real rewards of sobriety and the fruits of a spiritual life. For the man who wanted no family, no kids, no ties, no expectations from others, life was suddenly looking rich and complicated. What I discovered from my lengthy interview with Matt is that he couldn't be happier. Of course, he still has the freedom to do what he wants, but he has a wife, a son, a daughter-in-law, and two grandsons to share the freedom with.

And the truly mystical part of the story is that as Matt and Jerry, his son, shared the long and short versions of "their stories," Matt learned that Jerry had spent his summers three doors down from Matt's lake cabin for all of the years Matt and his wife owned that cabin. It was as though God was beginning to pull some strings on their behalf. Had Matt not called his sponsor after being confused by the suggestions offered by his friend, who knows what would be filling his life these days? But he has joy, peace, time, relationships that matter to him, and the excited voices of grandkids calling his name, all because he was willing to make some calls for the clarity he needed. He most definitely has become willing to believe "this outcome is a miracle."

We can see through the experiences Matt shared with me that the loving suggestions made to a willing listener—*and that's the key*—are guaranteed to change the events in one's life. It's not likely that Matt would have been thrown off his chosen, sober course for life by this new intrusion, even without the advice of others and his willingness to listen to the seemingly random suggestions made by friends. By this period in his life he not only wanted sobriety, but he wanted a peaceful existence. However, we can be fairly certain that the level of joy that now surrounds Matt might never have come to pass had he not asked, "What now?" after Jerry's existence came to light. Tom's comment "It's a miracle" was the perfect response.

AN ANTIDOTE TO ISOLATION

Sponsorship is such a gift, no matter who initiates it or what sustains it. We who share this program are specifically blessed that it is such an important part of our recovery process. The very act of being in the presence of another person in an intimate conversation is the antidote to the isolation that is one of the hallmarks of our disease. Each conversation, in fact, offers healing to both people. And the more each of us heals, the more we are able to share the details of what we have learned with the many other individuals who cross our paths. One and all, every person in every setting of life needs what we are learning and sharing. It is neither by accident nor chance that we have been called to this particular place and time to learn what we are learning. Nor is it an accident that we have become joined in this specific Twelve Step recovery movement.

The miracle of sponsorship is the theme of this book. It's important because we have so much to learn from one another in this rapidly changing world, and our "teachers" literally surround us. It's wonderfully miraculous to learn to acknowledge that wherever we are is where we are needed. That anyone we know and converse with, either seriously or casually, is there by design. Every "caller" seeks what our quiet inner voice already knows, just as the person we contact for help offers us a message that carries the lesson we are ready to learn or at least explore.

Sponsorship can take the guesswork out of our lives, specifically. In reality, it could take the guesswork out of the lives of the "normies" we may know, too. We generally come into the fellowship full of confusion and overcome by fear. If you were like me, you didn't want anyone to know you understood so little. Being told, often at one of the first meetings you attended, that getting a sponsor was absolutely mandatory if you wanted to stay sober was good news— scary news to many, but still, very good news. Had we not had this information impressed upon us, the comfort of the isolated life would have been far too easy to return to. Keeping company with only one's self is like living in a bad neighborhood. The dangers lurk everywhere.

What does a sponsor do for us that we can't do for ourselves? Among other things, sponsors impress upon us the importance of absolute honesty. Honesty is a necessity if we are to stay sober for a lifetime. Many of us no doubt thought we were honest, even as drunks, most of the time, but were we? How many times did you tell a little, inconsequential white lie to your spouse or your boss or your best friend or your son or your daughter when you didn't appear wherever you were supposed to be at the appointed time? That's the face of dishonesty.

Sponsors remind us that taking responsibility for our actions means being honest at all times, even when we don't want to be honest, even when our honesty might get us into trouble because it reveals our immaturity or our instability or our irresponsibility. Sponsors, when they are good, don't let us off the hook. They constantly serve as mirrors showing us who we really are. Without them, our growth would be stunted. And what we pass on to other people would miss the mark as well, because we would not have availed ourselves of our sponsors' knowledge and wisdom.

The spiritual growth we can attain in this fellowship is unexpected by many when they first "get here." But I have come to believe that it's the main reason for coming to this fellowship. For sure we all want sobriety or we wouldn't be here. But sobriety alone doesn't promise serenity. Most of us know this firsthand through the times we quit drinking without the help of the program or any other support group. We may have put the stopper in the bottle, but we were not able to feel the contentment that can accompany sobriety when we share the struggle and desire to stop using with the Power we discover is within us.

We learn about this Power from the men and women who were fortunate to have learned it before us. Their "calling" for the present time is to tell us what they learned and show us the way to find this Power, too. Our turn to tell others comes next. That's what sponsorship is about. We learn what we need to know, and then we tell others what they need to know. The constant reiteration of the same information, both telling it and listening to it, is what keeps all of us sober drunks sober. This process of sharing and listening is never finished. Thank God!

FOUR

WHEN THE STUDENT IS READY
THE TEACHER APPEARS

GLENDA'S STORY

Glenda was bombarded by so many excruciatingly painful lessons that I could hardly believe she lived to tell her story. But for some reason she was spared. Perhaps it was so she could share the story. Without a doubt it was also because so many individuals along her path needed her presence to give their own journeys new meaning. Our lives are intertwined quite purposefully.

Glenda grew up an only child, well cared for and well educated by loving parents. She spoke of her childhood as normal. Her father died and her mother remarried while she was in college, but drinking was never an issue in her family of origin. In fact, she could think of nothing in her childhood that could have enticed her to experiment with alcohol and drugs, but of course she found them anyway. At seventeen, she began to drink on a daily basis. By the time she was through college, she had developed dire health problems and was frequently under a doctor's care. Her introduction to Nebutal, Demerol, Percodan, and Valium were the result of the many doctors she consulted for her unnamed, though very present, illnesses.

By the time she was in her mid-twenties, she had under-gone five life-threatening, though very mysterious, abdominal surgeries, all of which baffled her husband (whom she had married after completing her master's degree) and her parents. Total confusion was the most apt description for the state of all of the significant people in Glenda's life. After her last surgery, which was complicated by her prescribed pain medications, her capabilities had deteriorated to the point that she was no longer able to function in the classroom. Her class of high school students was akin to a rudderless boat with her as the teacher. She was constantly dizzy and disoriented from the combination of pills she was taking. It eventually became apparent to her parents and husband that she was no longer employable. No one knew what to do with her or realized the extent of her drug use.

Glenda was committed to a psych ward in a major hospital, not once but twice, in the family's search for the cause of her problem. During neither stay was her addiction to chemicals detected by the august staff of physicians, so drugs were never considered as the root of her problem.

Fortunately, her cousin came to visit during her second commitment. He told her he thought she needed a different kind of help and suggested she go to treatment for alcohol and drugs. How this solution had occurred to him still puzzles Glenda, since Denny had never had a problem with either alcohol or drugs, but she heard his suggestion, more or less, and with the support of her family and her husband, who had been clueless all along as to her actual condition, she went to her first treatment for addiction in 1977.

SORTING OUT THE PUZZLE PIECES

Glenda's first treatment was little more than a reprieve from the daily dilemma she had been facing of how to take care of herself. Of course, as in most good treatment facilities, before her "graduation" counselors suggested she go to AA as the way to stay clean and sober, but she only half listened and attended few meetings after getting out. Her pattern of use and abuse quickly returned, as did her health problems. Outside of the safe environment of a treatment facility, she wasn't able to sustain sobriety for long on her own.

There were three more treatments before Glenda was to know what sobriety really entailed. Unfortunately, she had some harrowing experiences before she got to that point. Even though she had experienced a life free of pills while in treatment, she took them at random, and often excessively, as soon as she was released and on her own. There were always doctors willing to prescribe more pills; after all, she had had all of those painful and unnecessary surgeries, had become separated from her husband and was understandably depressed and distraught.

By the grace of God, she managed to crawl to the phone one evening after losing track of how many pills she had swallowed, in spite of the detailed record she attempted to keep every day. She somehow managed to make a crucial call to Judy, her best friend from college. Judy rushed to Glenda's side and took her to the hospital, where they immediately pumped her stomach. From the hospital she went to detox one last time. Judy was there to help her pick up the pieces when she was released. Even though Judy wasn't in a recovery program, she was instrumental in paving the way for Glenda to become willing to walk in that direction. By some, she might be considered Glenda's guardian angel.

Glenda once again agreed to go to AA, and she stuck around long enough this time to hear the messages that made a difference for her. The first came from Ross, an older man she talked with for three nights and three days, nonstop, she said. They went to his house for coffee following a meeting, and she noted that he subscribed to a magazine she also read. This tiny detail allowed her to think they had something in common besides having ended up in Alcoholics Anonymous, and this was the sign she needed to be willing to listen to his wisdom. First he listened to her, and then he talked, sharing his experience, strength, and hope. She felt, for the first time in her life, that she wasn't so different after all. Here was one person who understood the confusion she felt about the events in her life. Here was one person who didn't look at her with consternation and worry written all over his face. Instead, he smiled and nodded as she shared her journey.

TO BE KNOWN

She went home from Ross's house with a spirit of hope that had never before been known to her. Soon after, she met Joan, who became her sponsor and nearly constant companion for fourteen years. Joan "reeled" Glenda in. They shared meetings, entertainment, values, creative activities, books, and hours and hours and hours of talk. Joan listened and listened and then listened some more. Glenda had never before known the hope and the momentary peace that could come from simply being heard and understood. She had never lacked for love from her parents or her husband, but they had never known her as she was finally being known.

For the first couple of years in recovery, Glenda focused on little other than being clean and sober. She was employed, but not in positions that utilized her graduate education. She barely met her expenses. Program friends who had watched her miraculous change and growth suggested that she should consider helping others, perhaps as a counselor, since her own journey into recovery had been so rocky and traumatic.

She explored the educational requirements and eventually pursued a degree in counseling. This schooling moved her a great distance from her safe home group, but she had begun to trust herself and the program enough to believe that what she had found in the Northeast was available in the Midwest, too. Even though Judy and Ross and Joan were not moving with her, they were with her in spirit. This she knew absolutely.

From this point on, Glenda's journey resembles only slightly what her journey had been before. She was employable now. She went to work as a counselor after graduating and had the constant opportunity to influence others' lives in many of the ways hers had been influenced. She worked primarily with young adults, who mirrored her own troubled path. After working a few years in the counseling field, she grew restless, not for the excitement of drugs and alcohol, but because she felt that her real calling lay somewhere else.

THE TAPESTRY OF LIFE

Glenda had always loved the pursuit of knowledge and the life of a student. She had excelled in that role. It didn't confuse her in the way so many other roles had. Not surprisingly, when we consider how God works, she was soon to meet an individual who had just completed a Ph.D. in a field that fascinated her: American studies. And he was in recovery, too! They talked at length, and she came away determined that his field of study was the direction she was to go in. Meeting him in this unexpected way was a clear sign, she thought. Her sobriety had prepared her for this; she was convinced of it. When the student is ready, the teacher appears, and clearly, this man seemed to be that teacher.

She enrolled at a nearby university and began a new chapter. Glenda had maintained sobriety and freedom from drugs for many years; however, the ugly hand of uncertainty can grab us when we least expect it. Glenda found herself experiencing pangs of anxiety over her decision, her financial situation, and her future. But because she never failed to reach out to Joan when she needed guidance, her new home group when she needed personal contact, and her life of prayer when she was alone and scared, she survived the periods of uncertainty. She assured me that though she hit the wall many times, she was actually saved by her own willingness to give away what she had been given by so many individuals. Not just Joan and Ross and Judy, not just her former husband and her parents, but even her contacts at the university had taught her to believe in herself. No interaction is without its impact in the cycle of both participants' lives. Every contact is part of the tapestry of one's life.

Glenda continues to be sober and clean and finally abstinent from the food addiction that plagued her after her other addictions were addressed. She continues to work in higher education, the field that had called so loudly to her that she changed nearly everything in her life to pursue her Ph.D. But her challenges have continued. Her professional life, though rewarding, offers no guarantees. She is forced to wonder from year to year if her university position will be funded. This has resulted in a number of moves to homes that cost less and are generally farther away from her work. Yet, she is quite certain that all of these challenges have helped her to cement her relationship with God as she understands him.

She described it this way: "I feel free, more joyful and aware of God's presence than ever before. I lack nothing. I know that everything is possible with God. I have seen it many times!" Glenda's presence lights up a room when she enters it now, and just a few years ago she had been locked up, surrendered to the mental health system by a family who feared they would never be able to communicate with her again. Through all of her experiences, Glenda has come to believe that there is order in the universe. One example she shared was when she was absolutely penniless, in graduate school with no income, and the rent was due. She wondered how to explain her situation this time to her landlord. On the way to his apartment, she stopped by the mailbox and opened a letter from friends. In it was a check for a thousand dollars and a note that simply said, "We are thinking about you." She had not told them of her need and yet they somehow heard the prayer. This is evidence of the miracle of spiritual recovery. Glenda says her life is full of these instances, instances that she calls God's dancing lessons.

Glenda will no doubt be affecting the lives of others in the same positive way that her life has been affected for many years to come. She is certain, beyond a doubt, that you can't keep something that you aren't willing to give away. Her life as a recovering woman, a sponsor, and an academic professional is all about giving to others the wisdom she has been so gifted with. This *exchange* of information and love and acceptance is what keeps our recovery alive, not only in the Twelve Step program and among all of its adherents, but in the healing circle that is ever so gradually gathering in all of humanity.

It seems that most of us can't ever get too much of the mystery about how our lives have unfolded. We have been hearing ever since we came into these rooms of recovery that as each of us surrenders, more of the circle is complete. Our task, if we choose to take it up, is to foster the surrender of any person who reaches out to us for help.

WILLINGNESS TO LISTEN

I am relieved, and have been for nearly a quarter of a century, that I am exactly where I am supposed to be. Do you ever stop to reflect on this? If not, do so. Now. You and I are on a path that called to us. And in every instance, we finally listened, not necessarily willingly, to the suggestion of someone else that we needed help. There was the initial sponsor, the one individual who came to our aid even when we didn't know we were ailing. He or she was sent to us. Do you fully understand this now? And do you realize that you have been sent, likewise, on one or more similar missions to someone else? Even if you can't recall that first person you helped, her name or even her face, you have done your part. Doubtless, each of us has done our part on many occasions. That's what is so miraculous and mysterious about sponsorship. It doesn't have to be recognized as such, ever!

To reiterate, being a sponsor is about demonstrating our willingness to listen to the voices of those who seem to be troubled in our midst. It's about caring enough to say, very simply, how our own lives have worked. It's about being available when someone else is hurting deeply and needs an ear for listening or a presence to be close to. It's not about having to say the right thing. It's not about doing for someone else what they need to do for themselves. It's not about saving a life in a specific way. It's just about being—being present, being open and willing to listen, being an example of the helpful information that was passed on to us through so many experiences in our own past.

It's important to note that sponsorship involves no *musts*. Just as the Twelve Steps of AA are offered as suggestions, the role of a sponsor is as varied as are the many people who care enough to offer help. There are many ways to offer the help. Meeting for coffee and conversation is one. Helping the newcomer devise a plan for getting through a series of days, one at a time, is another. Praying together is not uncommon. The daily phone conversation is often necessary. Sharing with the newcomer how you did each Step, particularly how and why you wrote your first gratitude list or did your first inventory are invaluable, too. Let's never forget how overwhelmed we might have been when we first heard we needed to do a "fearless and thorough moral inventory."

I remember having no idea what "fearless and thorough" meant. I also remember being too ashamed to admit this to my sponsor. I didn't want her to know of my ignorance. So I spent dozens of hours writing seventy-five pages of history that detailed the actions of others, rather than my own actions. When I did my Fifth Step, the kindly gentleman I met with suggested that I had done a fine inventory of the other people in my life, but that I had failed to take into account my own behavior.

I walked home from our four-and-a-half-hour discussion crushed, embarrassed, and quite depressed. Had I humbled myself enough to ask for guidance from anyone else in the fellowship, I would have discovered what the inventory was really about. What I learned from this experience is to talk over the inventory with sponsees ahead of time, telling them my story and allowing them to ask all of the questions they might have.

Probably one of the most crucial things I learned early on was that the slogans, though simplistic and easily dismissed at first, were frequently the only suggestions I could absorb and follow. They kept me on the straight and narrow on many occasions. Now, after nearly a quarter of a century of sobriety, I turn to the slogans rapidly and often. I would even venture to say that I rely on them more now than in the early years. It seems that the longer I am sober, the simpler my perspective has become.

The slogans of AA are important: "First things first," "Let go and let God," "Keep it simple," "One day at a time." Every one of these and all of the others we have seen posted on recovery room walls can make any experience confronting us manageable. Helping sponsees understand the unmanageability of their lives before getting sober is doing them a great service. Then stressing how valuable the slogans have been in our lives is what really drives home their point. "Sharing our experience, strength, and hope" will make the difference. Pointing out how the slogans were shortcuts to our current state of peacefulness is some of the best education, the best "sponsorship" we can offer another person. We all know quite intimately our own successes and our perilous failures. Sharing them in any order is the substance of sponsorship.

FIVE

GIVE GOD YOUR WEARINESS

Pete began his drinking cycle when he was just a kid, but he "came by it honestly," a phrase my dad used to use about people whose behavior mimicked what they had seen at home. Pete's family of origin was no stranger to alcoholism. Miraculously, or perhaps unfortunately, Pete managed to accumulate seven DWI's with no concrete consequences. He stumbled along for years, creating havoc in his marriage. He was more or less an absent dad to his kids because he was in the bars and on the road for his job most of every week. As he tells it, for years it never even occurred to him that life might be lived any other way. He ran with a crowd of men who mirrored his own behavior. Like Pete, none of them had grown up with role models for doing their lives differently.

Pete's wife, Annie, though not overjoyed with his absences, didn't raise much of a fuss for years. In fact, she joined him at the bar on occasion, when she wasn't out drinking with her own friends. Theirs was a marriage held together by the glue of alcoholism and familiar dysfunction. This pattern continued until his oldest children were nearing their teens. Pete was growing weary of his life but was at a loss about how to change it. He was surrounded by people who lived each day in the same familiar pattern of hitting the bars early in the morning to get a handle on the day before actually having to greet it. When this is the way you have always done it, how can you even imagine there might be another way?

That's how Pete assumed he would live out his days, going from town to town, handling his business, hitting the bars first thing in the morning, at noon, and then again from midafternoon on until they closed their doors around him at night. It was finally becoming a miserable life, but he couldn't really imagine another option. And then one Thursday morning, as he sat at the bar, sick as a dog, drinking his usual, he began to ruminate about the emptiness he was feeling.

He suddenly knew he didn't want to live this way anymore; he didn't want to be deathly sick every morning, waiting eagerly for the bars to open. But he wasn't sure what that idea even meant or what to do next. All he can actually recall about that particular January 31 was that within that tiny, lone thought, he began to *feel* a new thought: *Just give it to God. Give to God the weariness you feel. Let God take over your life.* He looked around, wondering if someone had sneaked up behind him and said this. But he was alone, as he was on so many other mornings. He pushed away the drink, got up, and walked out the door.

That was Pete's last drink. But he felt lost and extremely scared. The next thought that came to him was to call the judge who had managed to "take care of" his seven DWI's. Surprisingly, the judge told Pete he needed to go to treatment. Perhaps even more surprising, Pete was willing. In fact, he was suddenly quite willing to do whatever someone told him to do now. Turning his life over to others gave him great relief. Just as the judge had managed to pull some strings to clear his driving record, he pulled a new set of strings now and got Pete admitted to treatment the following day. When Pete went home and told Annie what he was going to do, she scoffed. She had heard his plans to quit before. What Pete hadn't realized was that Annie had quit drinking on her own a month earlier without his even noticing.

Pete managed to refrain from taking another drink all day, but he didn't discard his pills. No one had even mentioned his pills to him, and he was addicted to many prescriptions. He stayed stoned on pills all day and went stoned on pills to treatment the next day. No one seemed to notice, or if they did, they ignored it. He had walked through the center's front door. That was the important first step.

GUARDIAN ANGEL IN THE FLESH

Fortunately for Pete, the counselor "God" assigned to him was the perfect choice. Herb was easygoing. He didn't demand that everything be done in a particular order. He more or less let the patient indicate the best order for his own treatment process. Herb wasn't a pushover; he was just very intuitive about how to handle the many different personalities who came into treatment. Pete is convinced that if he had had a tough, "you do it this way or else" kind of counselor, he would have run. He didn't like authority figures. That's why he had a job in which he was his own boss. His dad had been his boss for far too long. He wanted no more input of that type in his life.

He and Herb hit it off. They both understood where Pete was coming from. Finally, in the third week, Pete discovered that his pills had to go, too. He hadn't been taking them since arriving in treatment, but he had assumed he could resume their use when he left the facility. In one of Herb's lectures,

Pete learned that pills and alcohol were synonymous. They both altered one's mood and were off-limits to the individual who wanted recovery. Pete wasn't always sure he wanted life without pills, but he did know his drinking days had to be over. So he decided he could live with this. No alcohol. No pills.

A significant part of treatment for most folks is to do a Fourth and Fifth Step, a looking back at one's life. Pete was not able to do this in treatment. The pain was too great. The hurt was more than he could bear this early in his process of recovery. Herb let this requirement pass. For some patients this might not have been sensible or appropriate. But Herb knew there was another way to get to Pete, and they walked that way together.

Pete believed every word that Herb told him. Never before had he so fully trusted another human being. He wasn't even sure why this had become possible but thought it was because Herb seemingly had walked in Pete's shoes. They recognized in each other how similar their journey had been. Pete knew, in a silent sort of way, that Herb loved him and wanted him to live, that Herb was his guardian angel in the flesh.

When the time came for Pete to leave, the anxiety set in. He felt safe in the facility. He dreaded the drive home because he would have to pass Bunny's, the old haunt. Could he avoid turning in? He had never managed to avoid turning into their parking lot, even a single time, before he entered treatment. Herb wished Pete well, told him to go to AA, and said he was welcome back at the facility whenever he wanted to come. The door would always be open.

Pete managed to drive past Bunny's and get home. He breathed a big sigh of relief when he pulled into the drive. But what now? Going to AA sounded easier to do when he was in group or talking to Herb. Now he couldn't quite imagine it. But he was terrified of just sitting around. Herb had mentioned he was welcome back there whenever he felt like coming. And for the next ninety days, that's where Pete was, every night. Finally Herb, like a good sponsor, said, "Pete, you have to go to AA. Just pick a spot and show up." Initially, Pete felt betrayed. He had assumed he could just hang out in the safe setting of the facility. He wanted to continue to be welcome there, though, so he gathered up his courage and followed Herb's advice.

Because he didn't want to be recognized, he chose a group across town where he was sure no one would know him. How familiar this scenario is to so many of us. Somehow we convince ourselves that no one knew we were alcoholic and we don't want them to know now. What happened at Pete's first meeting is what happens to many of us. The first person he saw was his mailman! This was a good connection for Pete, because the mailman said, "You need a sponsor and I've got just the guy for you!" In the next moment, Pete was being introduced to Swanee, who immediately announced, "I am your sponsor and I will be taking your inventory!" Thus began a relationship that has survived for more than a quarter of a century.

For many of us, sponsors come and go. Not too infrequently, they even get drunk. But this sponsor/sponsee relationship had all the earmarks of a long-term relationship. Swanee was ever-present and he kept his word. He did take Pete's inventory on a regular basis. "What Step are you working? Why did you miss that meeting? Are you talking to your wife? What do you plan to do over the holiday? Are you prepared for the inevitable lows?" Swanee kept Pete on his toes. It surprised Pete that he let Swanee get close. He was used to telling very little to very few. But his dad knew Swanee, too, and so he trusted him, at least with part of his life.

He told me that without Swanee, he might not have made it. He was gruff and demanding, and Pete knew that he needed someone tough. But he also realized that he needed more than Swanee, so he kept going back to Herb. He could tell everything to Herb. Why he couldn't share everything with Swanee remains a mystery to Pete. Perhaps it was because Swanee knew his dad. Perhaps because Swanee didn't have that much more sobriety than Pete. At any rate, he recognized that he still needed an ear and feedback from Herb, and Herb never turned him away. From Swanee he got constant input about the "right way" to do the program. From Herb, he got the freedom to "make it work for you." Pete needed some of both.

One of the main things we must all learn is that having someone in our life, someone who can reach us when we prefer isolation, is what makes the difference between those who become "winners" and those who fail to make it. Pete had another person who came through when the times were tough: his dad. His dad had gotten sober before Pete, but his journey was a very different one. He didn't choose to take advantage of AA, although he did go to an occasional speaker meeting with Pete. Yet he knew the drill, and whenever Pete was struggling and wanted to drink, an idea that still called to him as a solution for many years into his sobriety, his dad was able to steer a new course for him. "Go walk around the lake," he would say. "The idea of a drink will be gone when you get back to where you started." Pete relied on his dad's advice countless times, and he has never had to take that first drink.

The biggest payoff in sobriety for Pete and for most of the rest of us, too, is the awareness of a Higher Power who is available in even the most mundane of circumstances. Pete had never quit believing in God, he said, but he had never considered seeking help or guidance from the God he had come to know as a youngster. Not until he felt God speaking to him at the bar on that fateful January 31 did he even consider that help was as close as the willingness to pray. Since then, he has grown used to prayer. And he has grown accustomed to a life of much greater peace and well-being.

POWERLESS OVER OTHERS' LIVES

But he struggled with the "peace part of the program" for many years, especially whenever confronted by the son who kept relapsing. One thing Pete discovered, big time, is that you can't give the program to everybody. No matter how your heart hurts for some people, they will not be able to heed your suggestions. This was the situation that Pete and his wife faced when trying to help their oldest son. Many treatments and many more relapses showed them just how powerless they were over another person's life. They couldn't have loved a person more than they loved their son, and they couldn't have tried any harder than they tried, but his sobriety and freedom from drugs was not theirs to control.

Pete was exhaustively challenged by his inability to make happen for his son what had happened for him, and he never willingly gave up his attempts to make his son stop using drugs and alcohol, but eventually his own sponsor convinced Pete to seek another perspective on the outcome of his son's life. When he was at last able to do this, the miracle occurred. And isn't this what we have known all along? When we finally give to God what is God's work to do, it gets done.

Pete couldn't be happier today. He has friends who really care about him now and a family whose members have become adept at nurturing each other. Pete and his wife have shared the program for years, and their son, after many attempts, finally shares the program, too. When Pete thinks back on his life and his circumstances some thirty years ago, he finds it nearly unfathomable that he has managed to make the journey this far, with the program as the solution to his struggles rather than with alcohol and pills.

The gratitude Pete feels for the intervention by the judge who arranged his admission to treatment, a man who really had no reason to care that much about him; and his involvement with Herb, the only kind of counselor who could have reached Pete, is awesome. He is convinced that were it not for these two "sponsors," he would not have lived to tell me his story or see his oldest son finally attain sobriety or create a loving relationship out of his forty-year marriage.

Those of us who make it, no matter how long it takes us to come to terms with the allure of alcohol or other drugs, feel so grateful to "have been chosen" to demonstrate the possibilities of this style of life to others. Fortunately our founders, Bill W. and Dr. Bob, understood that we can't foist onto others what we have discovered, but we can attract others to us by the changes in our own personality, our style of living, our willingness to listen rather than having all of the answers, and our improved personal lives. None among us is unchanged. Every one of us has a message to give and to show. There will always be times when our message goes unnoticed, as was true for a time with Pete and his son, but maybe at those times the message simply needs to be delivered by someone else. Thank God, someone else always surfaces. When the student is ready, a teacher will appear.

THE TWO-WAY STREET

Sponsorship manifested itself in Pete's recovery journey in Swanee, his first bona fide sponsor, as defined by the suggestions in the Big Book, but the judge and Herb are not to be overlooked. As I've mentioned earlier, anyone who helps us find a new path, who shares with us a new perspective for how life might be lived more serenely, has served us in "a sponsoring way." A *sponsor* shares experience, strength, and hope and offers suggestions; we learn by example. A sponsor doesn't have to be in the fellowship, as was proven by Pat's example, the woman who saved my life, but does need to offer us some new information that we are ready to hear and absorb and allow to become an occasion for change in how we live our lives.

Swanee had told Pete at their initial introduction that he was going to take Pete's inventory. That's not necessarily typical of a sponsor. However, a good sponsor will always give feedback, whether invited to or not. And a good sponsee will always listen, even when he or she doesn't want to. The exchange of information and the honesty of the interaction between sponsor and sponsee are what make the difference in both individuals' lives.

Sponsorship is a two-way street. Most of us who have been in the fellowship for some time are convinced that what we, ourselves, need to be reminded of will be asked of us by the sponsees in our lives. I have personally discovered that many times I didn't even know I was skating on thin ice with a certain issue until a sponsee called seeking help with a similar matter. It's miraculous how we can find ourselves giving to others what we need to receive.

Sponsors offer so many kinds of information. Not only do they tell the newcomer about the importance of meetings, but good sponsors stress service work. When most of us first come in, we aren't all that easy with talking about ourselves and the feeling of isolation, even in the setting of a meeting. Isolation is a condition to be avoided, even dreaded. It's the condition that kept most of us stuck for years. And when the way out of isolation is through sharing with others, newcomers can find themselves really fearful and unprepared for the process. Being told by a sponsor to come early to a meeting to participate in nonthreatening activities like setting up chairs, making coffee, and greeting other newcomers can be lifesaving. The simplest activity can be a turning point in the recovery of a newcomer.

Many kinds of information shared with a newcomer can serve as turning points. When my sponsor reminded me that principles should be placed above personalities, an idea I had been introduced to while reading the Big Book, I was saved from making a fool of myself. I was too new, too "green," to appreciate that what a person said, not how something was said, is what matters. I was too easily influenced by the glibness of some recovering people—in my case, men in particular. And I had not yet learned how to observe the walk, not just hear the talk. To learn how to really listen and watch how a person actually "walked" were paramount if I was to attain and maintain any long-term sobriety. Fortunately, I really wanted it and followed her suggestions.

Taking responsibility for all of our actions, those we would like to deny having occurred before we got sober and those that make us ashamed since entering the fellowship, makes the difference in whether we attain peace in this program or stay stuck in our old mind-set, our old way of thinking and doing and perceiving the world around us. Being responsible for every aspect and detail of one's life is empowering, but unless it's experienced, it's difficult to explain this concept to someone else. Sponsors can best show by example. Sponsors' very lives need to be examples, in fact, to the newcomers who enter our rooms.

Let's remember, however, that perfection is something we

only strive for. It's not attainable—not even by the person who has the most years of recovery in our rooms. Sharing the failures with sponsees is as valuable, some might say even more valuable, as sharing the successes. The operative word is "sharing." The lack of intimacy in the life of the newcomer prior to coming into these rooms was the key ingredient that kept the disease active. Isolation is deadly. It's the precursor to relapse. If sponsors can convey to sponsees only one thing, let it be that talking to others, to sponsors or friends in the rooms, will make the prospect of long-term abstinence not only viable but probable.

The reason anyone comes into the fellowship is that the need for change is finally acknowledged. In this respect, sponsors have so much to offer. But perhaps the most important idea to be shared, at least initially, is that even the tiniest change is significant at the onset of the recovery journey. It's common for newcomers to want big changes in their lives immediately. When finally confronted with the havoc that was present in their lives throughout the active using days, they are generally filled with shame and are highly motivated to "make everything right."

There is no harm in wanting to change the picture of the past, but it's far more productive to help the newcomer see that *what was* isn't *what is*. Conveying to them that incremental changes made on a daily basis are far more likely to take root thus fosters the long-term growth that recovery offers. If we can demonstrate this to the newcomer through our efforts to share how change was manifested in our own lives, we will have made the only contribution that is really necessary in our role as sponsor.

SIX

TIME TO SHARE WITH PEOPLE EVERYWHERE

HAROLD'S STORY

Harold's using had so completely absorbed his entire life that I was astonished he had the courage to recover. I have begun to believe, over the past twenty-four years of my own sobriety, that perhaps *courage* isn't the most adequate term. We will attain sobriety if we are *chosen* to attain it. And the sadness is that not all of us are chosen. In fact, many of us slip away, too many of us. But Harold was chosen and there are thousands, perhaps even millions, of people who, because of the work he does, have been or will be at a future time positively affected by his courage some eighteen years ago.

Harold's alcohol and drug use started when he was just a boy. When he first got drunk at age thirteen, the experience left a powerful impression on him and a high so dramatic that he sought that same "blast" of power again and again for nearly two decades. Unfortunately for Harold, he had a younger brother who was the "good boy." Harold never compared favorably with him, nor did he provide any reputable example for his brother, either. In fact, his brother eventually left home in order to escape the chaos of living in a household where Harold and his drugs ruled the behavior of others.

Harold was never a social drinker or even an experimental user of drugs. He did all of his using with a vengeance from the very start. Because his mother had a medicine cabinet filled with prescription drugs, Harold added these to his list of choices for escaping the reality of his life. The dangerous combination of chemicals gave Harold the feeling of being "charged up," a feeling he relished, a feeling that rivaled the first blast he had experienced.

It wasn't until the age of seventeen that Harold discovered marijuana, hashish, and LSD. He wasn't a daily user of these drugs initially, but because he gravitated toward other drug users in high school, he quickly lost all ambition about what tomorrow might hold for him. The idea of taking responsibility for himself and his future never crossed his mind. The only thing that did cross his mind was dread about getting out of high school and where the next blast was going to come from. Harold never got into serious trouble while in high school or he might have been forced to look at his path to destruction a lot sooner. Even though some may consider his avoidance of real trouble a miracle, perhaps it was, in actuality, a tragedy. The good news is that sobriety did beckon eventually.

Long before the beckoning to recover came, however, far more dangerous drugs beckoned, and he heeded the call. The older brothers of his high school contacts introduced him to heroin, and he quickly followed their lead. Even though he went to community college at his parents' suggestion, he went downhill very quickly. The combination of shooting heroin and drinking alcohol doesn't leave time for productive accomplishments. And the worst was yet to come.

Harold ended up in the hospital, one of many trips there,

as the result of an automobile accident in which he went through a windshield. He was introduced to painkillers in the hospital. He loved them—and they were legal. As he put it, "I milked the medical staff for all they were worth before getting discharged." Harold had a supply of painkillers he thought would last a long time. When they ran out, Harold, in extreme desperation, arranged a completely unnecessary operation on a nerve in his hand in order to replenish his supply.

"LEGAL" AND ILLEGAL DRUGS

At age twenty Harold overdosed on Seconal and was admitted to a mental hospital for thirty days. He considered it his good fortune to be reintroduced to Darvon, a drug he had earlier discovered among the many drugs in his mother's medicine cabinet. However, one doctor on staff suspected that Harold had a significant drug problem and intervened, suggesting that Harold enter a methadone program. That suited Harold just fine. Now he could get strong drugs legally.

Of course he took advantage of the situation and managed to talk the doctor, who obviously didn't really understand addiction, into prescribing Valium, Quaaludes, and an assortment of other pills. His ability to con others was very polished. For some time the doctor went along with Harold. Fortunately, he finally realized what was happening and cut off his supply.

Harold wasn't to be deterred, though. His mission was focused. He was streetwise by this time and became a daily user of Dilaudid. Shooting the drug was the most effective way to ingest it, and Harold paid others to shoot him up with either heroin or Dilaudid. He couldn't stand to shoot himself up, but he liked the high so much that he arranged another unnecessary operation, on his foot this time, to get the drugs he needed.

Harold, who was now twenty-five, was still living at home. His parents didn't really understand his problem or know what to do next. Nearly every year he ended up in a psychiatric hospital for a spell. He never remained clean after getting out. His drug addiction was never the focus of his hospitalization, and finally, after a number of hospitalizations, the medical staff even refused to admit him. They knew he would only come back in a few months and nothing would have changed.

During one of his last hospitalizations, Harold met the woman who was eventually to become his wife. After being released from the hospital, they moved in together, and used drugs together, but she held down a job in spite of this lifestyle. Her money quickly became his. If she didn't offer it willingly, he managed to steal it. Harold began stealing from strangers, too; he was arrested and went to jail before going back to the hospital one more time. He got two years' probation for the thefts and was considered a felon. But were his consequences enough to get him to stop using drugs? You can guess the answer.

His desperation for drugs, any drugs—heroin, cocaine, Dilaudid, or marijuana—took him to the more dangerous areas of town. He was beaten up on a regular basis, and the drugs he had just purchased were stolen more than once. Again he landed in jail but told his family and friends he had been kidnapped. Fortunately Harold was beginning to get scared about what was now happening on a regular basis. The beatings were brutal and he knew his life mattered not one whit to these dealers. He could see no way out of his situation.

The turning point for him came next. He quite miraculously started calling out for help to a minister, who, surpris-

ingly and unbeknownst to Harold, was in recovery from alcoholism and was a friend of his parents. He no longer remembers how he got the idea or the courage to call him at
that time, but fortunately he did. We probably all know where
that courage came from, and Harold realizes now, too, that
God was and is always at work. But at that time, God was certainly not on Harold's mind. However, the minister assuredly
can be considered God's special emissary.

PRISON OR TREATMENT

The minister and Harold's parents gave him two options:
prison or treatment. Harold settled for the latter, not having
any idea what treatment really meant. All he knew was that
he would be in a safe environment where he didn't need to
fear for his life. He also knew that he would be taken care of.
He would have no worries about meals or a place to sleep.
Harold arrived at his destination but had not an inkling of
what was to happen next. He suddenly felt scared, hopeless,
and lost, feelings not new to him.

That his life would begin to change was not imaginable to
Harold in those first few days of treatment. Twenty-eight days
of treatment was followed by a few months of extended care.
Harold was cut off from his family, his friends, his significant
other, and his drugs for many months. His family didn't seem
to mind at all that he was gone, so he willingly stayed. We can
only guess at how relieved they were to have him "incarcer-
ated" in a safe place. His counselor in treatment told him he
had to go to AA. Harold didn't like it much, but his options
were few. Go to AA or else, he was told. As is true for many
of us, he finds it hard to believe now that he resisted at first.

Fortunately for Harold, he met the man who was to become his first sponsor at that initial meeting. When, after

many meetings, Harold finally asked Don to be his sponsor, Don quickly replied, "Well, I am not going to baby-sit you!" Harold didn't really know what to expect from Don or why a sponsor was even important, but he soon began to find relief from his hopelessness and depression. For many months, he didn't really see how having a sponsor and the relief he was feeling were connected. The fogginess in his mind was not quick to leave. All he really understood was that when he talked about what was bothering him, he felt better. Harold was a long way from becoming the person he eventually became, but he was on the right path.

Next he got a job while still living in extended care. He hadn't really held down a job his entire life. He had had a small job here or there, on occasion, but most of his energy, since his early teens, had gone toward copping the next fix. Showing up for an eight-hour shift was unimaginable to Harold. Many who knew him then still laugh at the question he posed to his supervisor in the first week on his new job: "Don't we get to take a nap sometime during the day?" Harold wasn't kidding. Staying awake for eight hours straight was a difficult task for him. His mind was still so foggy from the years of Quaaludes, heroin, alcohol, coke, and so on that being alert for extended periods was not easy.

ANOTHER WAY TO LIVE

The one thing that Harold did stay alert to was what he was hearing at AA meetings. He had never heard the kind of information he was now actually able to listen to and absorb. He had never questioned why he used. Why he stole to continue using. Why he risked his life for the next fix, again and again. That's just how it was. Now he was actually able to see that there was another way to live, and he was getting the hang of it. He marveled at the fact that he was sticking with this program of recovery. He had never stuck with anything his whole life, not even Boy Scouts!

Don continued to be close to Harold. They talked regularly. And regularly Harold felt the tension in his life lessen. But he still feared that he was inadequate in some major way. Having dropped out of life from the age of thirteen until age twenty-seven, when he finally went to treatment, robbed Harold of the opportunities that could have shaped his personality and helped him to develop the self-esteem he was still lacking. He was too fearful to move beyond the only job he had ever held. Even though others encouraged him to try for jobs that were posted in his place of employment, he held back. For nearly seventeen years he held back.

But there were many ways in which he hadn't held back. He reached out constantly to his parents, trying to make up for all of the anguish he had caused them. He married the woman who had shared his experiences in the mental hospital, and she was strong and supportive and in recovery, too. Together they carried to others what they had discovered about learning to have a relationship. He was always able and willing to help others in trouble, no matter what kind of trouble. He never feared going out of his way to share his experience, strength, and hope. And he was always ready to go the extra mile on behalf of his own recovery. He learned early the benefits of sharing, even if he didn't understand what was actually transpiring at the time.

Virtually everything in Harold's personal life changed. And the years of sobriety kept accumulating. During his seventeenth year, he began to hear more frequently the refrain from others that "it was time for him to share with people everywhere what he did so well on a daily basis in his current job." At about this same time a suggestion was made by a manager that Harold needed to move up in the organization.

He was told that he wasn't doing all he could for the organization or himself or the millions of people who looked to this particular organization for guidance. Terrified of the responsibility a new position would foist upon him, Harold talked it over with his wife, his sponsor, and many friends. And he didn't forget to include God in his search for the answer. After many days of prayer and soul-searching, Harold said yes, he would apply for the new position. He knew he wasn't the only one applying, and he secretly rather hoped that another candidate would get the job. However, he did believe that God was in charge of the final outcome.

DOING FOR THE BIGGER WORLD

God made the choice. Harold was it. Now what? he thought. Even though he had a copy of the job description, he felt unsure of his new tasks on a daily basis. Again, his habit of talking to others about his tension and concerns saw him through this dilemma. "Just do for the bigger world out there what you do for all of us right here, every day," was one of the responses he got. Harold reflected back to the early days when his biggest challenge seemed to be to wake up enough to make it to and through a full day of work. Now his challenge was in figuring out how to transfer the "promises" as they had been fulfilled in his life to the lives of others who relied on this organization for guidance.

Little by little he realized he could do it. He could do it very well, in fact, if he remembered to make God his work partner. Harold claims God is his partner everywhere. In his marriage and every other relationship, too. One of the special gifts of his life now is that his parents have finally given him the recognition he had always secretly longed for but had no idea how to get. And his own mother has recently addressed her own dependence on prescription drugs. Who could have ever imagined, even a few short years ago, that he would someday be able to reflect the joys of this new way of life to such an extent that someone as close as his mother would decide to follow his example?

We simply never know what's in store for us when we become willing to turn our lives over to the caring hands of our Higher Power. Sobriety is only the beginning of what can be expected. New friends, new relationships, new family ties, new jobs, new thoughts, new perspectives, new hopes, new joys, new realities covering every dimension of our lives. And what did Harold need to do? Little more than become willing to do what his counselor told him to do and then follow the suggestions of his sponsor and the many friends he made in the fellowship. These were not extravagant assignments but they were the very tasks that made certain that Harold was in the right place at the right time to hear the next right message for his continued growth as a recovering man and as a responsible human being.

Those who knew him when he was young can hardly believe that Harold is the same individual. And he isn't, really. He has been transformed from the mere shadow of a person simply trying to stay alive long enough to secure the next needleful of heroin to a man who is dedicated to saving the lives of others. His guardian angels have been there all along. The minister comes to mind first. Without intervention, Harold wouldn't have made it to this time and place. And then the many people who followed his journey through these last eighteen years. The prayers of others combined with Harold's willing to listen have given us a man who is assuredly a wonderful example of what it means to be touched by the holiness of others.

Harold has turned his life over to the care of a loving God, and this has meant that he has continued to carry the message to others on a daily basis. It has also meant that he has been the sponsor that has made the difference in the lives of many others over these past few years. Were it not for sponsors, how many of us would be here today, reading this book? Had no one come to your aid when you were struggling, would you be here now? What kind of help did a sponsor give you? Did he or she do spectacular things? Perhaps. But most of us experienced the more ordinary things, the suggestions to go to meetings, to read the Big Book, to listen rather than thinking we had all of the answers. Some sponsors were even quick to say that we had no answers.

PRINCIPLES, NOT PERSONALITIES

One of the most important ideas I ever got from a sponsor was to focus on principles, not individual personalities. The fellowship can't promise us that every member will be honest, forthright, dependable, or even sober. It only promises us that if we look with our hearts and listen with them, too, we will recognize those who live a message worth our emulation.

Principles over personalities confused me a great deal at first. I was inclined to notice first how a person looked, and then I listened for the smooth, articulate responses to the topic in a meeting. I had not yet learned to pay close attention to how a person lived. Whether or not people walked the same walk they talked was beyond my understanding. But getting stung a few times because of assuming that others lived true to their words taught me valuable lessons. Were it not for the genuine guidance of seriously recovering people, few of us would live long enough to continue carrying the message. I remain grateful that my first sponsor said "Stopping drinking is merely the beginning." She also said, "Some folks who spout the talk have really gone no further than corking the bottle."

Nothing is demanded of us when we enter these rooms. Suggestions are made, but little more. Along with the suggestion that we read the Big Book, go to meetings, and not drink, we hear the message that we must take responsibility for our actions, past and present. We are able to observe how accountable others are being by what they are willing to share in meetings. This sharing, in turn, allows us to observe good choices for sponsors. How they "walk and talk" the principles of the program are the indicators we need when making a choice for a sponsor.

Choosing a sponsor is both a big deal and not so big a deal. By this I mean that many of us make a wrong choice initially. And nothing is lost by that as long as we don't stick too long with a wrong choice. Because we are so new to the fellowship, our first choice often mirrors the choices of friends we commonly made in our using past. The important awareness to glean from any choice is that we can remake our choices as we learn more about where we want to go in our sobriety as compared with where the sponsor seems to be going in hers.

Step One talks about unmanageability, ". . . and our lives had become unmanageable." One of the most obvious indicators of how well another person is working the program and thus how capable he or she might be as a sponsor is to note whether the person's sober life is chaotic or orderly. Does what she shares at a meeting reveal that she's walking a peaceful path or is she constantly in a state of turmoil? While it is true that every one of us experiences turmoil on occasion, *living in turmoil* suggests that a person isn't taking advantage of Step Three, ". . . to turn our will and our lives over to the care of God." It's not wise to choose a sponsor who isn't demonstrating the effects of using all of the Steps in his or her own life. The person who is using all of the Steps, most particularly the Third Step, is generally peaceful. It's that person we need to pay close attention to.

I have mentioned it before, but it bears repeating: the many individual perspectives shared at any single meeting constitute one of the most valuable revelations we will be introduced to in the fellowship. Each of us approaches this program differently, and each of us interprets what we read and what we hear and what we see a bit differently, too. And that is honored.

Often, in our family of origin, our differences were not honored, but they are honored in meetings. What we gain from this realization is the courage to see our lives from our own perspective, rather than trying to live according to another's perspective. We learn to trust our own hearts. Additionally, because we really care about one another in this fellowship, when any one of us perceives that someone is treading on thin ice, as revealed in what is being shared at a meeting or over coffee, we are supported through the program principles to share our observations.

Nowhere in the Big Book or other fellowship literature does it say that we should demand that a newcomer or an old-timer, for that matter, live the program in a certain, specific way. What we were told, what the Big Book specifies, and what the preamble stipulates is that we are here because we have the desire to stop drinking. Accomplishing this is done more easily one way than another, perhaps, but the freedom to choose our way is available to us, always.

SEVEN

An Attitude of Courtesy

Hadley came from a big Irish Catholic family who lived in the Midwest. Her father was an alcoholic, as were most of his twelve siblings. Her mother's role was similar to many women of her time and circumstance. She managed to bear most of the responsibility for raising the eight kids in Hadley's family on a daily basis, while keeping her eyes more or less closed to her husband's drinking. She didn't do this without making the kids suffer both guilt and anger, certainly. That was part of her payback for being the primary parent in this "good Catholic family" that showed up together, in a procession behind Dad, every Sunday morning for mass.

Each of Hadley's siblings, like Hadley herself, learned early on how to cope with a martyr for a mom and a drunk for a dad, one who was mostly physically absent, always emotionally absent, and seldom fully sober. Separation from the family, in some form, was the route taken by each of the eight kids. Hadley found her separation in alcohol at age fourteen.

The first time she drank, she violently threw up but was thrilled by it, anyway. Alcohol gave her the belief that she needed no one. In her own mind, she was God! Her arrogance and her sense of completeness made it appear to others, too, that she needed no one. At fourteen, Hadley assumed that the rest of her life would mirror the joy she thought she felt while drinking. She figured she had a hobby now, and she was glad. She had always heard her older brother say that everyone should have a hobby. He had one as a way for him to escape the pain of the family.

In 1969, Hadley's boyfriend turned her on to pot. Now she had two hobbies. And soon there were three and then four. She was willing to take any drug that came her way. Whatever was available was her drug of choice. She wasn't particular.

She moved to a part of the city where drugs proliferated. Her life became crazier. By age twenty-two she was in her third year of nursing school, having made that vocational choice because "wearing a white dress appealed to her." She lived on the edge but thought she was invincible. And then, in her words, "I experienced all of my stored-up feelings in one single afternoon." For some time she had sensed she was losing touch with reality and thought she rather liked it, that is until she had an episode in a grocery store that terrified even her. She got the shakes, could not make a decision of any kind, and ran screaming out of the store in search of help.

The help finally offered was a commitment to a state mental hospital. Her family reluctantly agreed this was best for her. No one had any inkling that drugs and alcohol were the precipitating problems. As far as they could tell, Hadley was clearly nuts. Her behavior was the indicator they used. The advice Hadley's parents sought from doctors substantiated their assessment. And all agreed that mentally ill people need to be separated from the rest of us!

The hospital wasn't a bright, cheery place. Its interior and the medical care that was provided matched the worst fears many of us harbor of mental hospitals. In this dreary setting Hadley's condition worsened and finally, because of her many suicide attempts while in the hospital, she was transferred by her family to an East Coast hospital that was better equipped to handle special cases. There she stayed for a number of months, receiving little clarity on her real condition but getting lots of opportunities for trying her hand at a number of meaningless crafts. The most positive aspect of the eastern hospital was that she was temporarily safe from the harm drugs had been doing to her body and brain.

With great effort, she began to appear well enough for release, and plans were made for her to return to the Midwest. She looked forward to her return. She had no plan in mind for the next phase of her life; she simply knew she wanted the freedom to exist however she chose. On the plane ride home, she got drunk on scotch. The nearly twelve months of incarceration, under a doctor's care, never suggested to her that alcohol was one of the problems in her life, nor had the hospital staff recognized the signs and symptoms of addiction.

In the fall of 1974, Hadley began working as a nurse. This was a fortuitous decision in her mind because she had easy access to all of the drugs she wanted. Stealing barbiturates was a no-brainer for Hadley. In reality, she couldn't work without them. She began concocting a mixture of speed and other drugs to shoot up. She was racing against time, and she didn't have a clue about where she was going.

The one thing she did eventually recognize was that her boyfriend needed help. His drug use was clearly out of control. He couldn't hold down a job. He could barely get out of bed. She took him to an outpatient treatment program not far from where they lived, and ended up staying for a while herself. The counselors there recognized immediately that

Hadley, too, was in need of help, but she didn't want help from them. Even though she stayed for a while, she left in a rage.

REACHING OUT

What happened next was a turning point. In desperation she called Bill, a man she barely knew but had met many months earlier when he worked for an agency next door to where she lived. His agency helped runaway kids. She wasn't sure what she wanted when she called him, but she remembered him as a thoughtful, caring, and gentle man, and she was confused and scared. He recognized the hidden request for help in her questions. He understood alcoholism and drug addiction very well. He had personal experience with both, and he suggested she go to Alcoholics Anonymous.

Miraculously, Hadley took Bill's advice. To this day she is surprised she was able to hear his suggestion and follow it. This wasn't her standard mode of operating. She had spent years resisting the suggestions of others, particularly when they ran counter to what she was currently doing. But Hadley was becoming a willing student, and the teacher appeared.

It was probably no accident that Bill had lived next door to Hadley, nor that the first person she met when she went to her first AA meeting was the individual who was to become her first sponsor. Although it is generally suggested that sponsors be of the same sex, in this instance no one could have been a better sponsor for Hadley than Charlie. She hated authority figures, and so did Charlie. He saw instantly how alike they were, and he said, "Do whatever you need to do. Just go to meetings, read the Big Book, and call me before you make any dumb mistakes." She heard him. And she did just as he said.

She looks back on Bill and Charlie as her angels in disguise. They appeared just when she needed them. Neither of them had ulterior motives for being in her life. They were just there, awaiting their assignment from God. Hadley dates her recovery as having begun during her interactions with Bill and then at that first AA meeting. Charlie and Bill were in her life for a purpose, as is true for all of us who walk this walk.

Hadley believes that sponsors play many roles in our lives. They show you how to work the Steps, which is necessary to clear away the wreckage in your life. By example, they teach you how to rely on your intuition. And they set an example for doing service work that becomes a must in remaining sober forever. Hadley said she didn't learn the specifics about God from a sponsor, but she could see and feel the importance of God in the lives of the people who became her sponsors. Even today, after twenty-five years of sobriety, she relies on the input of a sponsor quite often. Most recently her sponsor said, "How much quiet time are you building into your week?" She doesn't doubt that good sponsors will guide her back to where she needs to be if she calls upon them and listens to their suggestions.

Even though Hadley has long spells of serenity in her life presently, her road was often treacherous—scary and lonely and life-threatening. Hadley is the mother of two boys, one a teenager. She is married for the second time to her husband, Terry. Their marriage was initially built on passion. He is a doctor; she, a nurse. After she got sober, they solidified the relationship. He had children from an earlier marriage who were occasionally in their lives. The volatility was there from the first. It was part of the passion. Unfortunately, it was destructive to the relationship and his children. Gradually, the children pulled away and in time cut off all ties.

But with them gone, Hadley decided to have children of her own. It didn't appear that the marriage was in trouble yet, although the signs were probably evident to some. Hadley's separation from her husband didn't occur until their sons were seven and four. With the separation came constant turmoil: emotional, financial, and spiritual. Hadley had been diagnosed many years earlier with manic-depression, which was kept in check by medication, but she still rode an emotional roller coaster occasionally, and the boys were along for the ride. Their dad had his own set of problems at the same time, some financial, some emotional, but the spiritual despair was the most difficult.

The saving grace for the four of them were the Twelve Steps. Hadley never walked away from them, even when she was her angriest about the changes in her life. And her husband turned to them as well. Though the family was split for a number of years, the boys never lacked for involvement with both parents and a big extended family. Perhaps their current good adjustment is due to that set of circumstances. Neither parent failed to take rightful responsibility for the boys.

Although key people like Bill and Charlie had intervened at crucial times and ushered her into recovery and thus into a life of responsible actions, the next stage of Hadley's life was anything but smooth.

ANGELS ARE EVERYWHERE

After experiencing pain in her hip for a number of months, Hadley sought the counsel of a physician, but her own medical background no doubt prolonged her decision to seek medical help. Because she remembered pulling a muscle while working out, she was certain there was no cause for alarm. The doctor agreed, even though the condition had lingered. "The older we get, the longer it takes for an injury to heal," he said, and Hadley concurred.

But finally, after nearly a year, she sought a more intensive investigation into her condition. The prognosis wasn't good. The doctors determined she had bone cancer and immediately scheduled surgery. After nearly fourteen hours of surgery, Hadley had to wear a chest-high body cast for the next year. She went first to a nursing home before returning to her partially redesigned house. Her residence, where ever it was, had to accommodate wheelchairs, hospital beds, and a patient who was severely disabled.

Only a few weeks earlier, Hadley had assumed that her only problem in life was how to keep two rambunctious boys corralled enough to do well in school. Now she could barely feed herself and wheel herself around in a chair, let alone watch over boys their ages. She praises the recovery programs that came to her aid. "Angels were everywhere." Friends came at all hours of the night and day to prepare meals, keep her company, sit with the kids, transport them to school, and pick them up. Laundry, shopping, and cleaning were handled by others. So was the bathing of Hadley. Her only choice was to humbly put herself in the hands of family and friends and believe, somehow, that there were important lessons here for her and perhaps even for her boys.

Her anger over her condition subsided relatively quickly. Somehow she knew that with a problem as large as the one she had, only God could manage it. Hadley couldn't make her body do what it was no longer capable of doing. She couldn't bend or sit or stand. She could only lie flat, either in an extended wheelchair or on a bed. But she could pray. She could talk. She could laugh and tell stories. She could think. She could read and focus on what brought her joy. And most important, she could show others, by example, that peace

and happiness are available to us regardless of the circumstances in our lives. But what she did most was pray. She
prayed the same prayers over and over. Many of her thoughts
were too scary to dwell on, so giving herself up to the process of prayer was her ally.

Hadley learned very early in AA from Charlie and others
that intellectualizing a situation, any situation, didn't solve it,
nor did it offer much perspective. What the many "sponsors"
did tell her was that the best option for finding happiness
when confronted with any situation was to explore which
Step could offer insight or solace. In her present condition,
she had ample time to explore the hidden joys inherent in a
careful reworking of the Steps. She did this with relish. There
was, in fact, little else she could do right now.

One of the things she was soon to discover was that "living
in a chair" meant fewer distractions. Hadley, like most addicts, had always been easily distracted by the drama in others' lives, and when there was too little drama there, she
created her own. She had always been good at that. A manic-
depressive isn't always manic, of course, but when in that
condition, drama is cheap. Hadley was a drama queen, and
she knew it, but that appealed to her less now. Her life was
simpler, and she liked it. She didn't like how she got to this
point, but she appreciated things that she had never even
noted before.

Perspective and hindsight have allowed her to see that the
disease of alcoholism is far more devastating than dealing
with bone cancer, even though addiction took her down a
treacherous road for many mysterious years. Her exact
words were "Bone cancer is a piece of cake compared to the
disease of alcoholism." The pain of bone cancer pales in comparison to the pain of no people, no information, no contact,

no God in your life. At least that's how Hadley perceived it. Her spirit wasn't dampened by cancer. Fortunately she had been able to revive her spirit while addressing her alcoholism.

What had been the blessing in both diseases was that she had the intervention of others to help her face the unthinkable. The Bills and the Charlies were everywhere she turned when she needed them. They nurtured her through the scary times and strengthened her wavering hope when she wasn't confident that she could put her life back together. One of the miraculous outcomes of this whole experience was that her former husband made his entrance into her life again. He had never been far away. The boys had continued to see him on a regular basis, but now he was eager to offer his help to Hadley, too. And she needed him. She needed his help, his love, his support, and his presence on a daily basis in the evolution of their family.

What drew him back is open to speculation. Some in the family think that Hadley's father, who had died a few years before, had pulled some strings and helped two stubborn people see the light. That might be true. The important thing is that he came and she welcomed him and their family life attained a stability it had not ever had, even though they had both been working recovery programs nearly the entire time of their first marriage.

What was different this time might simply have been their awareness of God's closer presence in their lives, and they were primed to let God in. It's doubtful that many people are as primed as Hadley and Terry were. But having many years in a Twelve Step program teaches even the most stubborn among us that we are never alone and that we always have within us the solution to any situation that confounds us. We will always discover our solution if we quietly seek to know it.

NO MORE FEARS

Hadley says she fears nothing anymore. No longer does she see problems as insurmountable. She can navigate her home in a wheelchair. She can use crutches on those days when she has more energy and stamina. Her experience has totally changed how she sees the lives of her children, too. They are on loan to her. She says it's her job to treat them as kindly as she treats newcomers in AA. Even when they have destroyed a favorite possession, she asks her inner eye to see them as God sees them. She said this turnaround in her has changed them and their home life completely. God can be the disciplinarian. Hadley doesn't need that job.

She said she has learned that life is about learning to be courteous. Whether it's family life or her more public life, being willing to be courteous in every situation changes its outcome and thus the experience of every person involved in the situation—and eventually every additional person who is at some time touched by one of the original participants. The ripple effect goes on forever.

Perhaps an even more important discovery she has made since her life so dramatically changed is that the deep psychological conflicts she thought had to be dealt with in every marriage are no longer relevant, at least not in her life. An attitude of courtesy heals every relationship and each soul, from Hadley's perspective. She assured me that courtesy feels better in her body, too. In fact, she said she can count on her body alerting her when she isn't expressing the courtesy a situation deserves.

What she shared with me reminded me of the story I heard years ago about the Dalai Lama. He had been invited to speak at a prestigious dinner event in California. The wealthy attendees had paid heavily to hear his inspirational message. After finishing dinner, the moderator stepped to the podium and invited the guests to give a warm welcome to His Holiness. The Dalai Lama quietly walked to the podium, folded his hands, looked out among the members of the audience and very quietly said to them, "Your assignment in this life is to love one another." With that message uttered, he bowed to them, stepped back from the podium, and returned to his seat.

Whispering was audible throughout the auditorium. For what seemed like an eternity, no one on the stage moved a muscle. And then the Dalai Lama rose, walked back to the podium, resumed his position, and very softly spoke these words: "And if you can't love everybody, at least don't hurt anybody." With that final proclamation, he walked from the stage. Hadley was and is following the sage advice of the Dalai Lama, in her home and elsewhere, as much as possible. Her children are, too, and the result is astounding. In a home where chaos once reigned, peace is evident.

Hadley's story offers us, along with the drama, a solution that is available to all of us. If you don't ever take that first drink, if you do just as you are told by those who truly care about you, if you stay away from slippery places, if you willingly give back what has been given to you, if you listen with your heart and let it speak for you, you will recover from any condition. And you will know peace within any circumstance that entraps you.

Hadley, her children, and her husband have created a new family out of the old one that had not worked well. This new family offers itself as an example to others of what can actually work when the suggestions of "angels" are adhered to, when God is sought in every situation, and when you are willing to trust that no matter where you are, God is. In the body cast Hadley found God. In the cancer, God resided. And God was always in the marriage. Had Hadley not sought out Bill more than twenty-five years ago, she would not have found Charlie. They saved her, not the mental hospitals, not the doctors, not her family. And in that process of her being saved, perhaps a little bit of each of us reading this is saved, too.

Hadley's story tells us that you cannot possibly be certain of who is "waiting in line" to be your sponsor. All you can be certain of is that someone is there. God has not left us to handle our problems alone. Don't scoff at the suggestions that might come to you. Evaluate them with your heart. God may well be the messenger. Does this mean that every single individual is God's emissary? Maybe. We can't know for sure, but we can be certain that courtesy toward every person we encounter can be the invitation for a message to be shared with us that might make a difference in our lives.

Through sponsorship we learn about unconditional love. And we experience trust. While it may be true that some sponsors are more trustworthy than others, and a few even struggle to express unconditional love, we can at least practice these expressions in the context of the sponsoring relationship. Most important, a good sponsor will hammer away at the necessity of taking responsibility for all of our actions. Remember what Charlie told Hadley? "Go to meetings, read the Big Book, and *call me before you do anything stupid!*" Following that advice is taking responsibility for your actions before you go ahead and act. If we had not been told that by sponsors, how many of us would have embarrassed ourselves many times over? Perhaps we were not headed for a relapse, but going the wrong way down a one-way street always sets us up for eventual disaster.

Hadley's struggle with her family of origin, her marriage, her divorce, her cancer, and her permanent disability could have cowed many of us. Why wasn't she diminished? Likely it was because she never quit going to meetings. She never quit calling sponsors and friends. She didn't isolate herself. Even when she dreaded having others see her condition, she called out to them. Isolation will kill us, if not bodily, at least spiritually. And if we are dead spiritually, it's only a matter of time until the body follows.

Through our constant contact with others, we lose our fear and we develop our willingness. Without willingness, we make no progress. Even though our program is about progress not perfection, we are expected to make some progress on a regular basis, and the first step to making any progress is our willingness to go to whatever lengths our sponsors tell us to go to find the serenity that they have acquired and that is also promised to us in the program.

The root of our difficulties as human beings, whether addicts or not, is our desire to control the actions of others and thus the outcomes growing out of those actions. The slogan "Let go and let God" is a solution, a way out of our constant consternation. Hadley embodied this slogan more deeply as the details of her life worsened. But she managed with real humility and grace to let God have what was clearly his to handle. Her job, as she expressed it so succinctly, was to be courteous. She had learned that the rest would fall into place with her kids, her marriage, and her health.

A NEW PERSPECTIVE

If we actually practice letting go we will know a new peace because we will have freed ourselves from the constant need to control, a need that keeps a person agitated at best, fully obsessed at worst. Through letting go we will acquire a new perspective on our lives. We will be able to cultivate relationships that help us heal, and the healing of one of us contributes to the healing of all of us, in this fellowship as well as in the world at large. Having the fellowship as our family teaches us to offer what we learn there to the rest of our associations. That is how the world all around us begins to change.

Sponsors play a key role in exploring and experiencing the meaning within the many slogans written on posters that line the walls of the meeting rooms. I can certainly remember my uninformed reaction to those slogans when I first got sober. How silly and superficial I thought they were. I was convinced that life was far too complicated; that, in fact, it needed to be more complicated than the slogans suggested. How could "Keep it simple" and "Easy does it" have any real meaning for a life that was serious? It took a great deal of effort and a willingness I didn't always have to consider letting a slogan offer me the guidance I actually needed for the resolution of most problems. "One day at a time" couldn't be seriously adhered to, either, if we are contemplating a life with a future that must be planned for in order to get the outcome we want!

Yet what we learn is that most problems need little more than meditating on one of the slogans to put a problem in its proper perspective. One of the main things most of us lost in the years we gave to our alcohol and drug use was a healthy, clear, uncluttered perspective. Until we are willing to practice using the slogans, we can't know how effectively they will change our life.

It was helpful to me to listen really closely at meetings because I heard individuals I respected talk about the changes they were experiencing as the result of utilizing one seemingly silly slogan after another. I could see that slogans worked in others' lives. But I struggled to believe that my life was simple enough for them to work for me. What a long way we have to travel when first we enter these rooms. How fortunate for all of us that Bill W. and Dr. Bob had the foresight to realize that we needed traveling companions.

EIGHT

CONNECTIONS THAT HEAL

Larry seems bigger than life. At six and a half feet and 310 pounds, Larry quickly gains the attention of every person in any room he enters. The attention he gets now is primarily because of his size, but Larry has been getting lots of attention his whole life, partly because he was always bigger than the average kid, but also because he was prone to being in trouble: at school, with his folks, in the neighborhood, with the parents of his friends. His presence generally meant that chaos was on the horizon.

Larry liked attention as a kid. He liked it while in high school and the army. He still likes attention, and few escape getting caught up in his humor and his personality. He is one of a kind, you might say. And he is generally adored by all of his friends.

Larry's youth was misspent. He didn't distinguish himself in school, at least not academically. He did make a name for himself, however. He got drunk for the first time in the ninth grade, and this became a frequently repeated pattern. He became a serious shoplifter, too; a necessity, as he saw it. In order to afford drugs, he needed cash, and stealing whatever he could resell became his "work."

Although Larry didn't observe his parents drinking to excess, they were alcoholics and were preoccupied with their own drinking; thus he was able to avoid their prying eyes successfully. From about the ninth grade on, he figured he was on his own. He loved the freedom. He loved the booze. He loved the thrill of shoplifting. His partying lifestyle continued until he went into the service right after high school, a choice he felt forced to make after getting caught drinking when he was underage.

Like so many young guys then, he went straight to Vietnam after boot camp. After being there only a short time, his drug of choice changed. He still loved booze but he could function and do what was expected of him on marijuana, and it was prevalent. In fact, he was soon to discover that virtually any drug he wanted to experience was prevalent. Acid, speed, and even opium were readily available, and he became a master user of them all. He reigned supreme in his mastery for only a short time, though. As for every drug user, the drugs eventually became his master.

His experience in Vietnam seemed like no big deal to him. Being high made him fearless. He came back to the states to the girlfriend he had left behind. Her wish was to get married. He didn't really want to and avoided it for a time. But one night, while high on acid, he gave in to her pleas.

The first three years of the marriage were very rough. They never managed to celebrate even one of their first three anniversaries. They separated repeatedly yet stayed married until the kids were in school. The relationship was volatile at best and mean-spirited most often. To this day their marriage elicits extremely few, if any, good memories, and his contacts with his kids are few, too. The pain of the union scarred the whole family.

NOT SO SOCIAL USE

When Larry was about twenty, his folks went to treatment. He had confronted them, finally, when the family was experiencing real turmoil over his sister's abortion. His parents' alcoholism had made them unavailable to the family when it was in crisis; miraculously, they were willing to acknowledge that. Surprisingly, they had no reluctance about going to treatment, and it was an experience that involved all of the family. For Larry, sitting in the family sessions was the first time he got an inkling that his own alcohol and drug use wasn't "social." Much to his surprise, he kept hearing individuals tell *his* story when the group members, one by one, shared their stories.

Larry's dad's life dramatically changed with treatment. For his mom, the process has been much slower, but sober they have been ever since. After that family treatment experience, Larry, too, got sober a few months later, and has stayed sober ever since, but he didn't really recover from the disease of alcoholism for a number of years. Larry never chose to seek the help of AA or any other self-help program. He simply quit drinking and doing drugs and found that it wasn't that hard to do. He also realized pretty quickly that in many respects, his life was getting considerably better. He also noticed that most of his drinking friends were less fun now that he didn't drink.

AA had been suggested to Larry on more than one occasion, by his parents and then by acquaintances who were in the fellowship. Larry was quite open about his own alcoholism and had been ever since he was in the treatment center with his folks. But he didn't consider Alcoholics Anonymous relevant to his life. He was able to stay sober without it. Larry did become friendly with some men who were in the program, but they didn't push him to join them. We all know that joining the program happens best through attraction rather than promotion, but people are not always quickly attracted. Larry wasn't attracted at all until a number of critical events occurred in his life.

After his divorce, he met the woman who eventually was to become his second wife. He realized immediately that she was much different from his first wife. Her family was, too. He had never spent much time with people as cultured, as kind, and as well educated as they were. They related to each other in warm, caring ways. They talked to each other during dinner, too, not an ordinary experience for Larry. Being with Mona and her family gave him the opportunity to consider making a few necessary changes in his life. Even though he was sober, he still lived with chaos. He wasn't accustomed to living without turmoil.

After a period of courting, Larry and Mona began living together. She, too, was divorced with small children. Starting over with a new family was difficult, even though Larry was certain that Mona was the woman for him. She had a career and the drive to make a success of her life. She didn't need him to make her life complete. He realized, however, that she offered him a completion he had never before felt. She was a great teacher, perhaps the greatest he had ever had. Even though she began to understand alcoholism, she had been spared the worst of his disease. But as time revealed, she hadn't been spared all of it.

FACING THE DRY DRUNK

Mona eventually realized that alcoholism was an incurable illness that wore many faces, even in sobriety. Larry's behavior was often erratic at best, and not infrequently, wild and extremely unpredictable. Mona became confused and even began to doubt whether she wanted to stay in this marriage. Who had she married, anyway? Was he really the same person she had met and introduced to her family just a few years earlier?

What had occurred is what often occurs when an alcoholic chooses to get sober without the help of the fellowship and its suggestions for living the sane life. Larry was the embodiment of the perpetual dry drunk. He had maintained sobriety, but he hadn't escaped the insanity that marks alcoholism when left untreated. He didn't even recognize that he needed help. He did recognize, however, that the tension in their home was not pleasant.

His mother-in-law was on her way to their home for a visit, a visit Larry dreaded, and all he could imagine was how great it would be to get high on coke. He hadn't even thought about snorting coke for years, and now that's all he could think about. As he drove around in his car, full of anxiety, wondering what he was going to do, his wife was talking to his best friend about her concerns. She wasn't sure she wanted to stay in this marriage. For sure she didn't plan to stay unless some dramatic changes occurred, and fast.

When he got home, his terror at what he was contemplating triggered a call to his friend in recovery, Thomas, the friend who had always been there but who had never tried to pull Larry into the fellowship. Coincidentally, his wife had just called Thomas, too. Thomas wasn't surprised to get either call. He was only surprised that Larry had done it on his own, and not as the result of the urging of his wife. Thomas suggested Larry meet him immediately to go to a meeting. Larry wasn't really eager to do it, but he was desperate. He could see the handwriting on the wall—he knew he needed to make some significant changes. And he knew that he didn't have much time.

EVENTUAL SURRENDER

Larry didn't instantly take to the program, but he was willing to give it a go. After all, Thomas was a successful businessman, and he was able to admit that his life only worked well when he went to meetings. Larry wanted to have a life that resembled Thomas's life. He wanted success, joy, and a happy home life, and he didn't want to have to quit having fun to get it. It was apparent that Thomas still had a lot of fun, something that had always mystified Larry. For years they had been laughing and talking on the phone, daily in fact, and they socialized on the weekends. Fun was what Larry and Thomas and their wives had plenty of together. But for some reason, Larry feared he would no longer know how to have fun "if he turned his life over to the care of God."

Little by little, after surrendering to the idea of going to meetings, Larry began to change. He looked around at the men in his meetings and realized that others had been walking this walk for a long time. Why had he been so resistant? No alcoholic really wants to give up control, but when your control gets in the way of any semblance of peace in the home, giving up a little doesn't seem so bad. That's what Larry decided. Mona could see the changes, too. She was relieved.

As Larry reflects on his recovery, he is quick to give credit to Mona for giving him a reason to seek real recovery. She has been his best teacher, he assured me. Even though in the traditional sense she wasn't his sponsor, she certainly did offer Larry the important example of what healthy behavior looks like. He had paid little attention to it before. Even in his early sobriety before getting involved in the fellowship, he didn't notice healthy behavior often, except in the case of Mona and her family. They were his teachers, all of them. He is quick to credit his father-in-law for teaching him how to treat a wife. He had paid little attention to how his own mother was treated by his dad, and Larry certainly wasn't a good example of a how a husband should treat a wife in his first marriage. Now he had the teachers, but more important, he had the willingness to model new behavior.

Larry has relied on Thomas to be his AA sponsor ever since. Even though they had had daily phone conversations for years, now their conversations are full of the substance of what makes each of our lives better. Thomas talks and Larry listens. Larry talks and Thomas listens. Together they have improved two lives. Larry credits his dad's recovery with setting an example for him, too, when he was younger. Even though he didn't join his dad or his mom in AA, he was well aware of AA's availability because of their attendance. He just didn't think he needed it. He had been able to quit without much trouble at all. Staying quit with serenity is the key, however, and Larry couldn't do this well for very long.

The "angels" have been watching over Larry for a long time. Throughout his tour in Vietnam, during his many drunken escapades in a boat or a car, his life was spared. Is there something else he needs to do? He isn't sure. Are we ever sure? But he does know that he has learned more than he ever imagined possible about life, about being a father, a husband, a son, a businessman, and a sponsor. And he has not had to give up having fun in the process. In fact, he has more fun now because he knows there won't be dire consequences for his outrageous actions.

He closed his story by telling me about a friend of his who died at age forty-nine, a few years younger than Larry is now. His friend was diagnosed with cancer and died seventeen days later. His friend had it all. He was successful, had a great family, knew how to have fun, and had lots of it. He had been another of Larry's "sponsors." He was definitely a mentor in the world of business. He had always been there to help Larry solve his occupational problems. In seventeen days he was dead. He was dead before he had a chance to see his many friends and tell them good-bye. He was dead before he had a chance to let each one know how much they had meant to him, and, likewise, few of them had a chance to share their feelings about his contribution to their lives. His life was over before the reality of his prognosis could even set in. Larry took from this experience his most valuable lesson. He intends to have fun, to make sure his friends never doubt his love for them, and to be willing to give something back to another person every minute he is alive.

Learning from our lives, every detail of them, is the most worthy pursuit we can have. It doesn't really matter what we do for a living. Larry understands this with renewed vigor. What matters is how we do what we do and how we treat all of those people who cross our path during "our doing of it."

LIFESAVING CONNECTIONS

The most important aspect of sponsorship is that it can prevent isolation if the sponsee seeks the contact that is offered through sponsorship. Isolation is one of the hallmarks of our disease. And one of the hallmarks of our healing from this disease is connection with others—real, meaningful connection, the kind that happens when two or more are gathered together to talk intimately about the experiences in their lives.

This kind of connection can be initiated by either the sponsee or the sponsor. It can be done over the phone or in person. The main requirement is that the sponsee be willing to make the connection. He or she must be willing to see the necessity for the connection, although this seldom happens right away. In fact, it's generally necessary to offer our services as a sponsor to the newcomer and then encourage the follow-through for a period of time.

I always found it helpful to hear other people at meetings discuss their fears about calling sponsors when they first got sober. It allowed me to feel that I wasn't the only one who dreaded those early contacts. I never fully figured out what I was afraid of, but I suspect it was because I didn't want anyone, not even a sponsor, to know how messed up I thought I was. Pride has kept far too many individuals from asking for the help they so desperately need.

A very good friend of mine ended his life after about a year of sobriety because he couldn't let any of us know that he wasn't as good on the inside as he looked on the outside. Because he never told us who he really was, we had no opportunity to tell him what our own insides looked like. The tragedy is that Rollie's death is just one death among millions that result from this very same reason. We must let others know us, inside and out, and there is no better way than through the interaction that is encouraged in the sponsor-sponsee relationship.

Having a sponsor in one's life also means you always have an example readily available of how a situation can be handled. One of the rules of our program is that you have to give it away in order to keep it. This means that other recovering people will gladly offer to tell us how some aspect of the program helped them resolve similar situations.

We don't have to do what others suggest. We are bound by nothing in this program, but hearing about the successes of others when they experimented with using a particular solution makes it far easier to believe that we are deserving of the same kind of success, and then trying the same solution isn't so difficult. In fact, it makes sense to us in the vulnerable state we're in. Let's keep uppermost in our minds that the

Steps, the Traditions, and the principles as outlined in the Big Book are like a blueprint for living. Nothing will be too difficult if we follow the directions offered and listen to the suggestions made by a sponsor or another friend who readily understands both our disease and our struggle.

Saying the Serenity Prayer is the next best thing to having a conversation with our sponsor or another trusted friend. When no person is available to listen, prayer is always the answer. Prayer may well be considered the answer even when there are many others who can listen. God can hear us and will offer a solution that we will understand through the feelings we experience when we open our hearts. The fortunate element here is that the Serenity Prayer can be uttered any time, any place, while alone or in a crowded room, during intimate times with others or during periods fraught with fear.

When I heard the Serenity Prayer for the first time at the Al-Anon meeting I attended a few months before my own sobriety began, I was both astounded by the simplicity of it and astonished by the realization that the men and women gathered at this meeting believed it could help! It seemed far too passive an utterance to ensure that anything was going to change. At least that's how I heard it. I had come to Al-Anon to learn how to change others—now! The words in the Serenity Prayer didn't offer me the clear direction I sought for the changes in others I intended to make. I am grateful I didn't tell them how silly I thought their prayer was. I am even more grateful that I eventually found my way to Alcoholics Anonymous.

It was in those rooms that the Serenity Prayer became understandable and, in time, a lifeline. When I think back to my state of mind in 1976 and how ready I was to discard the slogans as too superficial and the Serenity Prayer as too passive to affect my life in any meaningful way, I have to smile.

Now I look to the slogans and this prayer as the obvious, ever-ready solutions for ridding my mind of the chaos that occasionally still creeps in. And once again I am reminded of how wise the founders and the other early members of the fellowship were. It's quite likely that most people who attain long-term sobriety or abstinence from other drugs have done so with the help of those very solutions I was inclined to ridicule and discard.

Frequent attendance at meetings is also another easy solution to any problem that troubles a person. I have heard it said many times that we will hear the solution to any problem we have at any meeting we attend if we go with our ears open and our minds willing to absorb the wisdom of others. Living the better life is so easy, really. It takes little more than an hour out of our day and the decision to quietly listen and willingly believe that the answer we need will be uttered by someone at the meeting.

After nearly a quarter of a century of sobriety, I have come to believe that a good sponsor insists that his sponsees attend as many meetings as they possibly can in the first few months of sobriety. It is often suggested, in fact, that a newly recovering person should go to ninety meetings in ninety days. If we put ourselves among those who have attained what we are seeking, we will attain it, too.

After all these years I still attend at least three meetings per week, sometimes four or five. I go to church every Sunday, and I belong to another spiritual group that meets weekly, as well. We cannot get too much spirituality in our lives. We cannot have too many healthy connections with others, the kind we get when we are in a gathering of others who truly love us. But we can get too isolated, too self-absorbed, too willful, too certain we have all of the answers. And when we are *there,* all answers will evade us.

NINE

FINAL DESTINATION: SOBRIETY

HELEN'S STORY

Helen's life as an addict was well hidden and drawn out over many years. Her profession made it possible to keep her addiction under cover for a long time. Helen was one of three kids in a model family: upstanding, church-going, apparently quite happy. But the family wasn't really what it appeared to be to onlookers, and Helen was the first to discover this when she walked in on her mom and their minister in a compromising position. Helen, though mortified and very shaken, kept their secret. However, the word got out eventually, and Helen's mom left home, taking Helen's little sister with her. Helen chose to live with her humiliated father.

Helen's drinking began on her first New Year's Eve after high school graduation. Her first introduction to Thunderbird wine was a thrill. Alcohol made the subsequent parties even better, but she didn't let her drinking get out of control until after her first marriage at age twenty-three. From that point on, it quickly got out of control. But since she didn't drink until noon, she fooled herself into thinking otherwise.

Not surprisingly, Helen repeated her mother's pattern of

infidelity. She had her first affair with a co-worker. After getting pregnant by her husband, she broke off the affair. When her children were eight and nine, Helen was introduced to marijuana by a friend, and she immediately loved it; her life soon revolved around it. Because of the turmoil in her marriage, which ultimately led to divorce, and the turmoil with her growing kids—in fact, the turmoil she was experiencing with every aspect of her life by now—she sought the help of a psychologist. She admitted to him that she used drugs and that she couldn't imagine existing without one in particular: marijuana. In reality, she couldn't imagine even wanting to exist at all without pot. Helen had a nervous breakdown. Burning the candle at both ends had finally caught up with her.

Helen was no longer married, so when she met a young man while in the lockup ward of the local hospital, it made perfect sense to her to bring him home. Helen didn't realize, initially, the severity of Todd's addiction. She simply knew she felt sorry for him. She thought he was cute, she had a big house, and he needed a place to stay. When she got him home, she was actually surprised to see how consumed he was by drugs. As she watched him shoot up for the first of hundreds of times, she felt a stab of fear. What would happen next? She never really knew the answer to that question once he had moved in, and that became the torment. Meanwhile, she exposed her children to great turmoil.

During the first few months of their cohabitation, Todd introduced Helen to Darvon, which she grew to love as much as she loved marijuana. In due time it became easier to get Darvon than marijuana because she worked at a pharmacy and had daily access to prescription drugs. Helen had never imagined she would become a thief, and although she managed to avoid admitting it to herself, a thief she was. She cov-

ered her tracks well, however. Because she had worked in the
pharmacy for a number of years and because her employers
respected her, they never suspected what she was doing.

THE TABLES TURN

For a couple of years Helen measured her use and apparent
well-being against that of Todd's. He was very strung out by
now, so she rationalized that *she* had no real problem. His
journey was about to end, however. His choices were getting
fewer. The law was after him, and so were his parents. They
finally convinced Helen that Todd needed to go to treatment
and he needed her support. She supported him in his treatment, but her own drug use escalated.

With Todd in treatment, Helen suddenly felt free to use
all the drugs she craved because she no longer had to worry
about what he was going to do next. With him out of the
house, her "baby-sitting" chores were over. What she had not
counted on was that Todd's parents would want her to go to
the family phase of the treatment program with them. They
had recognized her importance in Todd's life, though not her
drug addiction. Helen had assumed she would never see Todd
again when he left for treatment, and she was growing accustomed to that idea. Their request surprised her.

Helen agreed to their wishes and arrived sober for her
participation in the family portion of the treatment program.
But as soon as her commitment to them was over, she rushed
back to Illinois and to her drugs. Her abuse of drugs became
excessive now, much as Todd's had been before he went to
treatment. Soon she was living reclusively in a flea-infested
house. Eventually, her drug of choice, Darvon, turned on her.
She ended up in an emergency room because of an allergic

reaction to it. She survived the reaction and weaned herself from Darvon, but she didn't consider giving up the rest of her drugs.

How she ended up in Al-Anon remains a mystery to her, since she was still using drugs daily and even went stoned to her first meeting. But she showed up nonetheless. No doubt we all have experiences like this that we can point to. Someone, somewhere makes a suggestion and we follow it, without any clear understanding of why. At the time, the suggestion hardly registers on our mind, but we take the information in. Later, we are apt to see that moment as a significant turning point in our lives. An "angel" had descended, and we had succumbed to her charm.

After being in Al-Anon for a while, Helen returned to the treatment center to experience the family phase again. Mysteriously, she still didn't recognize her own addiction. Thus, she didn't quit using. In fact, her use was so all-consuming that her kids had become, out of necessity, her caregivers. Even though she was barely existing from one high to the next, she surprisingly, and suddenly, made a geographical move that was to set the stage for her eventual recovery. She relocated to her present home, leaving her children, who were now young adults, with their father in Illinois.

Before moving, she finally confronted the question of her drug use. She knew she had no choice but to quit if she were going to be close to Todd. Could she do it? The question haunted her, but she was determined to try. Shortly after moving to her present home, she and Todd married as planned, but it wasn't wedded bliss. Helen stayed sober, as she had promised herself she would. However, sobriety took its toll on her. Even though she wasn't using chemicals, she clearly needed help. Her rage over her life—over the past, the present, and her future without drugs—consumed her.

She kicked Todd out. He seemed to represent her rage. In reality, of course, her untreated addiction was the cause for her rage.

THE RIGHT TIME, THE RIGHT PLACE

Had Helen not met Rachel at about this time, she might have given up and returned to Illinois and the using life she had previously loved and now missed so much. But because she had continued going to Al-Anon, she met Rachel, who was an alcoholism counselor. Rachel could see there was something else wrong with Helen besides her codependency. After a few conversations, she understood what Helen's real issue was and told her that Al-Anon was important for her serenity but wasn't going to help her address the specific and more pressing problem, which was her own unrecognized, untreated addiction.

How did Rachel pick up on this so quickly? The signs were certainly evident. Since Rachel had dealt with so many other alcoholics, she wasn't easily fooled. Rachel was certainly an angel in disguise, like the many "sponsors" who enter our lives. She respectfully ushered Helen into the AA program and has remained in her life ever since, constantly serving as a reminder to Helen that we are always in the right place at the right time. Al-Anon had been that "right place" for Helen; even though she had never considered that she was an addict needing help, and even though she had been among recovering people throughout her marriage to Todd, it was the intervention of Rachel at this particular time that made it possible for Helen to find her *next right place* and the serenity that had been eluding her.

Helen worked her way through the Steps, and with her sponsor's help, she got in touch with all of the shame of her past: the shame about not being present in her kids' lives at crucial times, about missing their performances at school because she was too high or too caught up with Todd's addiction to notice that they were counting on her. She had shame about her first marriage and her many infidelities, about the rage she had carried so long toward her mother, about the prescription drugs she stole from the family-owned pharmacy where she had worked for so many years.

When she shared with her kids the news of her sobriety and told them of her sadness at missing out on so many important events of their lives, they forgave her. Their immediate and unconditional love sustained her until she could begin loving herself. It took a while for her shame to subside enough to make *feeling* their love possible.

Helen vigilantly worked on her sobriety and on her ability to love herself and others. And she consistently attended meetings of both AA and Al-Anon. As her confidence grew, she began to explore other career opportunities. She had never forgotten the service Rachel had performed for her when she suggested that Helen consider her own using history. In quiet times, she found herself nurturing the idea that she, too, might be able to intervene in the life of someone else as a way of paying back the world for what Rachel had done for her in asking Helen the questions she needed to be asked.

When Helen talked her idea over with her sponsor, she suggested that Helen should consider going to counselor training. Helen doubted that she could get accepted, but she was determined to throw her hat in the ring anyway. Then when she was accepted, she doubted that she could do the work. But she could and she did, although it didn't come easy to her. Fortunately through it all, she had the support of Todd, who was now comfortably experiencing his second decade of recovery. Both of their families, who were clearly grateful that Helen and Todd had found each other and had been able to walk this path together, were supportive of Helen's decision, as well.

One of the blessings of sobriety is being able to look back on our journey and relish how far we have come. Helen looks back on her journey every day. As she works with new patients who are seeking what she has come to enjoy, she can share with them the gratitude that awaits them. She knows they will find it and feel it. It comes to everyone who wants it. She has learned, as we all have, that there were no accidents in her life. Yes, she may have been able to avoid particular incidents, but the final destination was sobriety. She does not doubt that for a single instant. She shares with patients repeatedly that whomever they have met along their path played a role that was crucial to their getting to this point in time. Helen lovingly tells them about Rachel and how she directed this most important passage in her own life. She tells them about the miracles that have occurred in her family of origin, about the forgiveness that has occurred between her and her mother and her and her own children. She promises them that they will experience the same blessings, and that they will come to love every person who ever made a mark on their lives.

Helen helped to impress upon me the absence of coincidence in our lives. I love the phrase I have heard so often repeated at meetings and from my own sponsor, that "coincidences are simply God's attempts to remain anonymous." It gives me such comfort to know that God is never absent, and my comfort level rises with the awareness that I will never be confronted with a situation that I cannot handle as long as I seek the support of my Higher Power, who may well be best accessed when I make a call to my sponsor. We all get wonderful messages from our sponsors. The key is deciding to recognize the *real* origin of the messages and then trusting them.

MANY ARE CALLED

Some say, "If only I had known where I was going." I have come to believe that had I known, I would not have relished the journey that has blessed me in hundreds of ways. We simply can't know what's going to be best for us. We can only know that God will make sure it is offered to us. Many resist, of course, and they end up in an obituary column. "Many are called but few answer," or so I have heard. That's why it is incumbent upon those of us who have answered, to do the work of the many who were called. That means be there, as a listener, a way-shower, a storyteller, a traditional sponsor, a friend, a silent "partner," a willing participant in the life of whomever is in your presence at any moment in your history. Not an easy assignment, you might say, but there is none more rewarding.

Many individuals are able to contribute in "sponsorly" ways to our journey without actually being members of our fellowship. Even though other members of the fellowship may have a clearer understanding of the particular stumbling blocks we might encounter, they aren't the only sources of wise advice.

When I think back to my own experience with Pat, the woman who literally saved me from suicide, I would have to say her advice was invaluable to me. Without her presence in my life, you would not be reading this book right now. God doesn't discount the potential value of any person in our experience. Nor should we. God is willing to use any of the people in our lives for a greater purpose than they might have imagined for themselves. Those of us in the fellowship are frequently reminded that we are on a mission with a greater purpose, but how often do we remember that all members of the human community are likewise on that same mission?

Take a moment to reflect on your encounters with other people in the past week. How many of them were with members of the fellowship? No doubt some were, but certainly not all of them were. Do you appreciate the fact that all of the rest of the encounters were with men and women appointed by God to enter your life at that very moment? When I remember this awesome fact, when I remember that Pat knocked on my door at such a specific time for an appointment that I had no recollection of setting up, I doubt not that God is in charge, and with a master plan that weaves all of us in a vast, meaningful tapestry. Let's rejoice in this awareness. It can mean the difference between trusting in the present and the future or being terrified by the unknown. Nothing is unknown to God. Never forget that.

Being confident about the unknown is a trait we can observe in others. And it's an enviable trait. Even though we have been told repeatedly that God will never lead us where he isn't willing to protect us, we often tremble about the steps we need to take. That's when we need to call a sponsor to remind us of the safety of our journey.

Choosing a good sponsor can be agonizing for some of us. Many of us take far too long to make the decision. Perhaps some of you reading this have never had a sponsor. If that's the case for you, is it because of your fear to ask or your unwillingness to let someone else know that you aren't perfect already?

I well remember my first sponsor. I asked her because she had four years of recovery when I came in. She always seemed to be surrounded by people who looked up to her. Whenever she talked, she mentioned how closely she listened to God whenever she was confused. And she was willing to admit that she didn't always understand what was going on in her life. That I was terrified of calling her to tell her I was confused, too, didn't make sense. But that was the case. I wanted her to think I was all put together, that I didn't really need a sponsor. Sound familiar to you? I hope not too familiar. I have considered many times that I might not have reached the point of a planned, and nearly accomplished, suicide had I called her all the many times I really needed to talk to her.

Having support, the kind that is close and very personal, between meetings is mandatory if one is to continue making progress. Surely reading many of the recovery books will help us recover. So will going to meetings, some would say the more the better. Certainly most of us would advise going to more than one a week. I think that in the early days of recovery, well-being is directly proportional to the number of meetings attended in a week. We have all heard about making ninety in ninety. We cannot go to too many meetings in the early days. And when we find ourselves in the muck of our lives at any later time in sobriety, a really good sponsor will or should suggest, "Go to ninety in ninety."

When choosing a sponsor, keep your choice simple. Don't analyze this too much. You can always switch sponsors. Your choice doesn't have to be for a lifetime. You are not marrying this individual. He or she will be your guide in working the program. Look and listen for your sponsor's wisdom. A sponsor need not share all of your values, need not have all of the answers, need not share your profession, your style of dress, your neighborhood, your ethnicity, your age range, or even your gender, although sticking with our own gender, at least in the early days of sobriety, is best. Sponsors simply need to be willing to listen, to be honest, and to share with you their own experience, strength, and hope.

Sponsors can show you how to live by example. But they don't have to answer every call you make. They may not always be available, in fact. Remember, they have busy, demanding, and sometimes troubled lives, too. At those times, go to God. Or perhaps consider having a backup sponsor. Or you can simply call a friend or rely on your own intuition for a change. After all, you have been educating your own inner voice ever since coming into these rooms of Alcoholics Anonymous.

You probably shouldn't count on keeping the same sponsor forever. As you grow and change, so do your needs. Your sponsor will have grown and changed, too. Be aware of this, and don't get too anxious if you see your needs no longer being met by him or her. You can handle this awareness by adding an additional sponsor when your own life or your sponsor's begins to change. Or you can simply let the sponsor you have go altogether. Sponsors seldom fret over "being fired." Good ones generally have so many other sponsees that having one less might actually be a relief, as long as the loss isn't due to relapse or death. The guidelines for the decision to change sponsors is to be kind to yourself and to do what is best for you. Your choices are what count, not only in this situation but in all situations you experience on this journey.

TEN

A DOCTOR WHO MAKES HOUSE CALLS

JAMES'S STORY

Crack cocaine nearly destroyed James's life, not just once but many times. He is now professionally successful, articulate, well-groomed, a loving husband and father, the son of proud parents, and capable of influencing the lives of hundreds of thousands of people with his own recovery. It's hard to believe that just five years ago he was hiding in a crack house, not caring whether he ever made it out alive. But he was rescued. It wasn't the first time he had been rescued, but that time was perhaps more important because he had a recovering wife who needed him and a disabled child who was suffering greatly because of his absence.

In his youth, James certainly didn't imagine he would travel the path he has taken. He was born into an affluent home. His parents were well educated and professionally accomplished, with prominent political ties. It was common to see their names and pictures in newspapers. James often had the good fortune to be in the company of well-known philosophers, politicians, and historians. He took these experiences for granted. After all, many people considered it an honor to sit at the feet of his own father. But he recognized from the time he was a youngster that he wanted attention, lots of it, and he was bent on getting it regardless of what lengths he had to go to. Just being the son of well-known parents was hardly enough attention for James.

He told me he felt as if he had a hole in his soul. A hole that couldn't be filled by normal encounters with people. He never felt accepted, even in places where he clearly belonged. He was a prime candidate for addiction, and that's the path he took, starting in his early teens. But before going down that path, he had a couple of experiences I want to share with you because of their significance as hallmarks for "one of us."

The first one was as a youngster playing, while barefoot, in the yard by his grandmother's house. There were many bees in the yard on this summer morning, and his grandmother warned him to avoid them. After she had gone back inside the house, he watched carefully for the bees. When he spied three or four in the grass close by, he slowly crept over and stepped on the one nearest to him. He screamed bloody murder. It hurt far more than he had imagined, and his grandmother came running. The pain was great, but the attention he got was worth it. A pattern was set in place; James became willing to go to extreme lengths for attention.

A few years later, after school one afternoon, he was hit by a boy in an altercation. He wasn't hit very hard, but he pretended to be knocked out. He was intent on getting all of the attention and sympathy he could. He succeeded in fooling the others, but he knew, deep within, that something wasn't right about this behavior, although he didn't understand what.

At age fifteen he discovered marijuana; smoking it began

to soothe the big hole he felt inside. He smoked pot regularly and secretly and without detection or consequences. His relationship with his family was still good. They had no idea he was smoking pot. Nor did they know he suffered as the result of the empty hole inside. His parents continued to believe their son was going to make them proud in every detail of his life. James didn't pursue other chemical substances until he got to college. Marijuana had kept him on an even keel for quite a while. But with the experience of college, coupled with his fear of not getting the attention he craved, the drinking began. It began with a bang. His first episode with drinking was a binge, and that's how he characterized his drinking all of the way through college.

AN ABERRATION

At age twenty-one, one particular binge placed him in a dark alley after downing twenty-one shots of whiskey, wetting his pants just prior to breaking a store window. He was arrested. He had no idea where he was, what he was doing, or why. The window was there. So was he! His arrest was publicized in the newspapers. His parents were completely baffled by this occurrence in James's life. They were absolutely certain it was an aberration. They had never seen any sign of this kind of behavior before. Of course the behavior had been there all through college. It just hadn't reached the newspapers.

James suffered from severely low self-esteem. He always had, but he didn't know how to characterize this to others. He didn't really understand why he felt so inadequate. His parents had always been loving and supportive. His dad had served as a mentor for him, putting no unreasonable demands on him, ever. But the fact remained that he never felt that he belonged or that he was as good as all of his buddies and acquaintances. He did well enough in school in spite of this, but his pain was overwhelming at times. The binges helped, as did the other drugs, but only momentarily.

He then discovered cocaine. He felt as though real help had come at last. Cocaine did for him what no other drug had done so far. It transported him from wherever he was to where he wanted to be, in just a few short minutes. It was at about this time that James married his childhood sweetheart. She never knew about his drug use; not once in the eight years they were married did she suspect that his first love was cocaine.

He was a busy journalist and reporter, on assignments constantly, making it easy for James to keep her in the dark. But he knew he was using drugs far too much. He recognized how fried he was from the drugs. However, his co-workers, like his wife, were unaware. He continued to turn in work that was good and on time. His need to please other people was so great that he frequently worked overtime to make sure his work was beyond reproach. Until he hit his first bottom in a crack house in Harlem, no one knew that James had a hidden life—no one but the crack dealer who told him to "smoke the stuff" if he wanted to hit the fourth dimension. He did smoke it, he did hit the fourth dimension, and he crashed.

CLEANING UP THE PAST

When James first went for treatment, he and his wife separated. That was in 1989. Twenty-eight days of treatment wasn't enough for James. He needed more time away from the allure of drugs, so he went into a halfway house upon graduation from treatment. It was in the halfway house that he met the woman who was, in time, to become his second wife. They became good friends, and helped each other find joy in sobriety, but James had a lot of his past to clean up before he and Teresa might consider anything more than a friendship.

He returned to New York for "the cleanup," and Teresa joined him after the cleanup was completed. They moved in together and soon married, but it wasn't long before he had returned to his old haunts and his using life. Living "on the outside" wasn't like living in the halfway house. He wasn't safe from the call of this outside world even though he lived with a wife who was in recovery. His vulnerability made him an easy target.

His relapse came in 1990. He had clearly been told that sponsees needed guidance and could count on it from sponsors, and he had gotten a sponsor after getting out of treatment. But he failed to act in his own best interests when he needed to make the call to Ted, not an unusual choice for someone bent on using drugs again.

He slid into the same heavy use of drugs that had been his pattern before treatment, and he eventually ended up back in the crack houses. He couldn't stay there forever if he wanted to stay alive, however, so he resentfully went back to treatment in 1991. His idea was "to teach that treatment center a lesson!" He reasoned that it must have been his counselors' fault he wasn't able to maintain his sobriety.

After getting out of treatment the second time, he did stay sober, though angrily so, for three years. He and his family had moved to another large city, where he was able to get work in the journalistic field. He wasn't at peace, but he was working and he stayed sober until shortly after his wife gave birth to a child with special needs. He was no doubt looking for an excuse to return to the life he loved best, and this was

a good one. He didn't deserve a son who was less than perfect! That, coupled with boredom, made him an easy target
once again for a relapse. Initially it was short lived. He told
his wife what had happened, and she was willing to help once
again, but he wasn't able to maintain his sobriety for long.

THE UNTEACHABLE EGO

He went to detox and before getting out, his caring sponsor
flew in from Minnesota. They were able to have only one
hour together. He told James to put his ego aside. James
wondered aloud if there was any room for the ego in a sober
life, and Ted wisely said, "Only if it is teachable." Unfortunately James's ego wasn't yet teachable. Not long after leaving the detox center in September 1994, he journeyed back
to the crack houses. His clinical depression was part of the
problem in this relapse, but the rest of the problem was
simple. He was a drug addict and he wanted to smoke crack.

His next crack house visit was an extended one; he went
in with money and groceries and stayed. Had an angel of
sorts not intervened, he likely would have died in that house.
To this day, he says he "was delivered" from that place. No
one really knew where he was, not even his wife; they only
suspected he was back in the crack neighborhood. But the
chairman for the news corporation that employed him had
methods for tracking down a person. James was discovered
and his "delivery" was facilitated. He knew he had the option
of staying, but a part of him really wanted to survive. He left
the crack house and returned to detox, where he was on suicide watch for eight days.

While in detox, on October 12, 1994, he heard a voice
just as clearly as though it came from a person standing next
to him. The voice said, "Saint Paul." He was convinced that it

meant he should return to his earlier treatment center. His wife agreed, and he surrendered to the treatment center yet again. But the surrender was different this time, or at least he thought so. He finally felt that he was ready to go to any lengths to get better.

One hundred and fifteen days later, he felt ready to return to his job in Atlanta. But that job didn't fit him well any more. The pace was one he couldn't sustain without the high of cocaine, and he felt he needed a change of scenery. Before long, he was drawn back to Minnesota, this time not for treatment but to begin life again with his family and in a new career.

VESSELS OF GREAT WISDOM

Since his return to Minnesota, James has had numerous occasions to put into practice all of the suggestions that had been made so many times before by sponsors, suggestions that he just didn't take time to really listen to and certainly never adhered to. He is convinced that sponsors are the channels, the vessels, he calls them, for great wisdom. They offer up "liquid knowledge." And James was eager to drink from its cup this time. He has also been eager to share his recovery experience with others. His main sponsor told him years ago that secrets keep you sick. James wants his health at long last.

James should have been dead so many times. The trips to crack houses, alone and in neighborhoods where few dared to tread, were clear invitations for disaster, but repeatedly he was spared. He is certain that he lived because God had other plans for him. He travels the country now, not only sharing his experience, strength, and hope, but sharing the history of this wonderful fellowship that has saved so many of us. His voice and his knowledge are sought and cherished. His message continues to save others' lives, just as he was saved.

We never know what the future may hold for us. Certainly James had no idea what lay in store for him as he nodded off in one crack house after another, not caring if he ever emerged. But the journey is only partly ours. We make decisions, certainly. We make mistakes repeatedly. However, we will get to our destination in spite of ourselves. James is living proof of this. We all are living proof of this. We may take a number of detours along the way, but we cannot be deterred forever. Thank God.

We often hear people in the program say, "If I had known years ago where I was headed, I would have run as fast as my legs could carry me in the opposite direction." I, too, once could not imagine living a sober, drug-free life, and certainly did not want to. It would not have seemed like living to me. I know you understand what I mean, but here we are, and for the most part, we are happier than we ever imagined possible.

REALIZED HAPPINESS

We found the serenity of recovery as the result of someone, generally uninvited, who made the effort to intervene in our lives. That someone might have been an employer, a spouse, a friend, or a son or daughter. In some cases, the interloper might have been a total stranger but one we had "messed with," with the outcome that he or she initiated the action that was to change our life. It really matters very little why we got here. That we got here wasn't an accident. Thus our current happiness isn't an accident, either.

I have given a lot of thought to my happiness in the past few years. Perhaps this is because the happiness that I now feel eluded me so often in the first few years of my sobriety. I still ponder why I couldn't relax and enjoy the constant presence of God. I was able to believe intellectually, after Pat had intervened on my planned suicide, that God was present in my life, that there were no coincidences, that "I was always in the right place at the right time." But I still didn't feel the gift of God's presence in my body. I was tense most of the time. I was still waiting for the other shoe to drop. I was quick to anger and even quicker to feel the inner turmoil of fear. My anxiety often prevented me from joining a group of friends who were having fun. I was still outside the fishbowl, not so different from when I was living my addiction.

The up side of my anxiety and struggle to know God was that I sought solace in writing, and fortunately found it there. The books that carry my name are the result. I have frequently laughed that had I felt as good in early recovery as I feel now, I would never have written *Each Day a New Beginning*. But the important fact is that I didn't give up seeking. Nor have you, if you are reading this book.

My assumption is that much of your seeking was with the help and guidance of a sponsor. Aren't we lucky that the disease we suffer from promises us a doctor willing to make house and phone calls every time we request help? Perhaps you had to be coached into believing this when you first joined the fellowship, however. Most of us did. I can well remember wondering if my sponsor would think I was a sicko if I called her too often. I wasn't sure how often was appropriate. I didn't ever ask her what she expected of me as a sponsee. I can't remember asking my first sponsor much of anything, in fact.

There is no right way to work with a sponsor, and there is no instruction book. The simple fact is, the antidote to our disease, no matter how long we have been sober, is to join with others. Be a sponsor, call a sponsor, or just be a friend and be willing to listen and share your own experience, strength, and hope, regardless of how old or new you are in the program. When any two are gathered together, God is present to make it three.

One of the questions that is often asked is, How long do you have to be in the fellowship to become a sponsor? There is no set amount of time. You can be older than your sponsee or younger. You can have more sobriety or less. The key is, does the person you are thinking of "joining" with have a need you can fill as a sponsor? Or if you are the sponsee, does the potential sponsor have a program you admire? We can't really make any long-term errors in our choices or in our responses when called upon to act as a sponsor. Nothing has to be forever. Our main assignment, as a sponsor, is to be helpful, honest, and kind. Our main assignment as a sponsee is to decide we want help. Neither is difficult once we decide we want a different kind of life.

Every person I spoke with for this book had found sponsors to be invaluable in their recovery. And many, like myself, found that a certain individual outside of the fellowship of Alcoholics Anonymous had truly "sponsored" them on their way to a new path for life, even though the shift in direction or the impact the shift would eventually have was not evident at the time of the encounter. When I reflect on this, I am convinced that the tapestry of our lives is being woven for us by a silent partner. The lucky among us come to understand and cherish the knowledge of who the weaver is. And we also cherish the knowledge that simply every person who crosses our path is there by design and is carrying a message, or part of a message, that we need to know and make use of for the proper unfolding of the rest of our lives.

ELEVEN

LESSONS THAT COME
LIKE METEORS

PETER'S STORY

Peter grew up in a religious home in the Bible Belt, but he didn't enter adulthood a spiritually centered man. He was confused and frightened until he discovered alcohol. It was only in college that he made that discovery, but when he did, life began to take on a different hue.

Because of his drive to excel, Peter didn't let the alcohol take over his life at first, although he relished his first sip of sloe gin. His number one priority was to have a successful career, a goal he was sure to achieve, given his drive and focus. Alcohol became a must in his life, but he was so motivated to succeed that he remained a high-functioning drunk for years.

When his drinking got out of hand, Peter was able to stay dry for periods of time. He once stayed dry for two years, and was fairly comfortable throughout that time. He actually enjoyed the excitement of not drinking. Was it perhaps because he knew he would return to it when he was ready, and not before, thus keeping alive the thrill of drinking again?

You might ask, Why did he return to the use of alcohol at

all? Alcoholics can't really explain to anyone's satisfaction why they return to drinking. They just do. And as most of us have come to believe, alcoholics will always return to drinking unless they are committed to doing what each of us reading this book has made a commitment to do: get involved in the fellowship of Alcoholics Anonymous or some other equally valuable program that offers support.

Peter had several avenues to travel before he was ready to quit drinking. To his alcoholic advantage, he had a number of techniques in place while on the job that allowed him to function efficiently in his high-powered position. For one thing, he had instituted rules that had to be explicitly followed in any meeting he was expected to attend. An agenda had to be preapproved by him, and he had to be told in a detailed way what was expected of him. In this way, of course, he could mask the fact that he was losing touch with the business in general and his decision-making responsibilities in particular. His fear of being found out grew. Peter wasn't sure what the problem was, but when someone fortuitously suggested that perhaps he needed to quit drinking, he was willing to consider it.

In fact, a short time later, Peter did make the decision to address his drinking several months prior to actually doing anything about it. He called a treatment center that was close to his home and made an appointment for an arrival date seven months from the date of his call. He then proceeded to tell his friends of the appointment and his plan for sobriety. He instinctively knew, he said, that telling others what he planned to do was a good idea.

The last few days before going into treatment were wild ones for Peter. He drank nearly nonstop. It was as though he were trying to finally get his fill before relinquishing his role as the drunk. When at last he entered treatment, he quickly questioned his decision. He was sick as a dog at first, and he hated treatment. He hated the rules. They weren't his rules. He hated his counselor for wanting to change his life. And he was astounded that he was surrounded by people who were not drinking and who didn't seem to be bothered by not drinking.

The weeks quickly passed. He learned more than he had bargained for. He moved from excessive grandiosity to actually revealing a hint of humility. He had become teachable. He had adjusted to the rules. Upon leaving treatment, Peter got a sponsor, a man with a generous soul who worked the program assiduously. He was available and able to help Peter work the program seriously, too. Peter tried to remember every day what his counselor, a man he had finally grown to love before he "graduated," had also told him: "Don't bleed until you've been shot."

NEW PRIORITIES

Peter's return to work was a difficult transition. He no longer had the drive to do the demanding, creative work he had been so eager to do before. The work seemed so pointless now. He had discovered in treatment that life was full of fascinating possibilities that had never drawn his attention before, had never even occurred to him in fact. His profession seemed so trite in comparison. Fortunately for Peter, he had a good sponsor, one who was able to help him sort out what was important for him to do and what wasn't. Together they decided that it was time for him to leave the position that he had worked so hard to attain.

From high school on, he had been driven to excel in his field, but that meant little to him now. It was okay to walk away from the work that had initially given him so much prestige, financial gain, and creative fulfillment. What he sought now couldn't be found there. His sponsor helped him see that. Sponsors are more than just our friends and guides and AA teachers. They can serve as our eyes, our ears, and even our hearts until we have rediscovered all three of these ourselves.

And where is Peter now? He remains clean and sober and full of gratitude for the many teachers around him. He says that what he needs to learn comes at him like a meteor, just as his sponsor assured him it would, and if he ducks the impact, it will come around again. These days he is devoting his life and his creativity to organizations and causes that speak to his soul. The forces for change and enlightenment are present everywhere, and he is constantly listening for their call and nudging himself to be teachable. He is adamant about living in the moment, being vulnerable to the moment, and staying open. None of these absolutes were available to him before he joined us on our path.

Most recently he has gotten a new sponsor who is reaching him in ways he had never been reached before. Peter loves the simple solutions even though he has always been a ready victim of the more complex ones. Victor, the new sponsor, "cuts through all of the crap" with simple questions or an occasional statement. "You're dragging your coat, Peter. Pick it up." This was Victor's way of telling Peter that he was pulling himself down, nothing more complicated than that. Peter could hear the message. Peter could *see* the message. And he felt profoundly understood.

Having people in your life who are willing to name what's going on, who have no investment in whether you really like them or not, is valuable. The truth will set you free. That sounds dramatic but I do mean it. The alcoholic can always find so-called friends who will lie to him. Finding the person who is willing to speak the truth is what may save one's life.

Peter had been fortunate to find a number of these individuals along his way to sobriety. Many of them he didn't like at first. His counselor comes quickly to mind. But what Peter learned and shared with me in our brief time together was that he knew the forces were always present to get any one of us back on the right path. We could ignore the invitations, the many signs to change our direction, some obvious and others quite subtle, but we could never erase the call to us that was being made. It would come, again and again, until we became willing to listen to it.

Since recovering, Peter's perspective toward life has been profound: *Be here. There is enough time.* In a wonderfully unexpected twist on the theme of this book, Peter has acted as a very special sponsor to me. I was told many years ago by my first sponsor that one can always tell when an "angel" has spoken by the goose bumps that appear on one's arms. When Peter spoke those words to me, which I now pass on to you, I knew they came from my Higher Power. The messengers are all around us, every minute of the day. You are God's messenger, too. Never forget this.

RECOGNIZING GOD'S GRACE

I am constantly reminded that God is doing for us what we have not been able to do for ourselves. Many of us have been plucked from the depths of despair simply because of God's grace. Our part has been our willingness and little more. Doesn't it give you an overwhelming sense of gratitude to be able to reflect on your survival, a survival that for many of us was against all odds? Pat, the woman who knocked on my door nearly twenty-three years ago, was one of God's angels on assignment. My work was far from done. The same must be true for you or you wouldn't be here now, either, willingly searching for what may be in store for you next.

One of the avenues that is open to each of us every day is to offer a helping hand to someone else. When I first got sober, I was consumed with my own program and couldn't imagine helping someone else. However, my perception of what constituted help was pretty distorted. I am very much aware now that I was helped by many people in tiny, quiet ways, not ways I even thought of then or even now as "sponsorly" in the way we use that term in the fellowship. But these helping hands were a form of sponsorship.

Often I am simply overwhelmed by the profound understanding our founders had about the value of personal communication, not just talking but sharing the deepest intimacies of one's own life. Had this not occurred between Bill W. and Dr. Bob more than sixty years ago, we might not be here now. I have pondered hundreds of times over the years how they knew what they needed to do to stay sober. I think we must conclude that the answer is that God was doing for them what they could not have done for themselves, *all alone*. And God is doing the same for us right now, just as he has done for everyone who has shared a story with me.

You may be wondering if it's time for you to be someone's sponsor, if you haven't assumed this responsibility yet. What you are agreeing to do, when asked to be a sponsor (or if you have offered to be one, though unasked, as is appropriate on occasion) is to

- be available to discuss problems with the sponsee
- have a willingness to share personal stories that are pertinent to the sponsee's problem
- make a suspension of judgment on what the sponsee shares
- promise strict adherence to confidentiality regarding all matters that are discussed between the two of you

Without both parties being at ease in the discussions that need to take place, real help gets skirted. Probably the most important quality you bring to the sponsorship table is your personal evidence that things will change for the better. Any sponsor is a symbol in the flesh that hope will replace despair and fear will be a memory rather than an everyday, paralyzing reality.

No doubt the biggest fear most new sponsors have is that they don't know enough to be a good one. Dispel this belief at once. You don't need to know facts or figures regarding alcoholism or drug addiction. You don't need to know the intricate subtleties of the Steps or traditions. You don't even have to know the Big Book in detail. Those who glibly quote the Big Book are not necessarily the best sponsors, nor are they always the most serene or the healthiest.

Just knowing what the book says doesn't mean a person has changed the way he or she lives. It's specific information about how to change that sponsees seek in a sponsor. To be a sponsor you only need to know your own story, your own failures and your own successes, because that is what you are going to share with the sponsee, in the hopes that she or he can learn from your mistakes.

SHOW BY EXAMPLE

Your main assignment is to show by example what has worked for you, how your life has changed as the result of utilizing certain program principles in your daily life. No one among us wants to be told we have to do something. But most of us are willing to hear how another plan of attack might work.

For many of us, the help we receive will be or has been nonspecific on many occasions. That kind of help is equally

effective with some individuals. The foremost problem for alcoholics, for every member of the human community, for
that matter, is the authority problem. Not one of us wants to
be controlled. Not one of us wants to be admonished for
doing something wrong. And certainly, not one of us wants to
be told there is only one way of doing something.

The "Easy does it" slogan is good advice when it comes
to addressing our issues in recovery with our sponsors or
friends. As a sponsor, offering just a little bit of information
to the sponsee regarding a particular problem is enough at
first. No one needs to change overnight. Not one of us got
here after only one night's worth of drinking or drugging,
did we?

Another important slogan or piece of advice for the
sponsor to impart to the sponsee is "Don't think!" When I
first entered the fellowship of Alcoholics Anonymous and
saw Don't Think! on a meeting wall, I almost turned around
and walked out.

To be told to not think seemed ludicrous! It also seemed
dangerous; it reeked of mind control, and I wanted nothing
to do with a program that wanted to take over my mind.
Fortunately, I got some input from some of the old-timers,
my sponsor in particular, before I bolted from the program.
She and they told me that the slogan meant simply this: "My
best thinking has brought me here. Perhaps it is time to let
others think for me." I couldn't argue with that explanation. I
stayed. I am still here and grateful to be here.

The paramount piece of information a sponsor can give is
that the strength necessary to handle any problem is available
from a Higher Source, a Power greater than any one of us
alone and greater than all of us together. Demonstrating how
that has been true in the sponsor's life is the key that can unlock the wall of fear the sponsee has built around herself.

Unfortunately, it won't always unlock that fear immediately. The next person I spoke with continues to struggle with fear, which in his case is generally expressed as anger. Anger can be our undoing. You have certainly heard by now that alcoholics can't afford to have resentments. Nor can we hold on to anger or fear without those emotions impeding the progress we have been promised in the Big Book of Alcoholics Anonymous.

TWELVE

KEEP TALKING, KEEP LISTENING

DAVE'S STORY

Unfinished business from our past will prevent our present from being what we deserve it to be. Dave is a good, though unfortunate, example of this unofficial axiom. While still very young, Dave tried to block out the pain in his raging, dysfunctional family by drinking.

By the age of seventeen, he was suffering from near constant blackouts, which convinced him he was crazy. He tried to commit himself to the state hospital, but because of his age, they sent him to a psychologist. He diagnosed the problem as being in Dave's head and prescribed Valium. Dave assumed that Valium was indeed the solution, and for a time it seemed to help. Then he had a frightening experience with the medication, so he flushed the remaining pills down the toilet.

He was soon back on the merry-go-round of drinking accompanied by blackouts. Finally he decided to quit drinking. For three and a half years he was off liquor, but he felt miserable. After this experiment with abstinence, he went back to the only behavior he knew the conditions of: drinking.

He married his first wife in this state of "dis-ease." Their

entire sixteen-year marriage was troubled by Dave's alcoholism. No doubt his anger contributed to the breakup of the
marriage, too. Dave wasn't ready to consider alcoholism
treatment as a cure for his drinking yet, even though his pain
was acute. But within the time frame of his second marriage,
a marriage that was also troubled by Dave's anger as well as
his drinking, he was finally, though reluctantly, willing to go
to AA with a clergyman friend. Much to his dismay and surprise, he knew most of the people at the meeting. Naturally
he didn't want to stick around. He certainly didn't want
them to think he had a problem with alcohol.

Fortunately Dave did eventually go back. He listened to
the old-timers at the meeting, men who told him what it was
like, in effect, to be him. This astounded Dave. He had never
before experienced being understood by another person. He
had not grown up in an environment where this had occurred. His father was an extremely angry, resentful man who
also drank too much and who talked very little to anyone,
except to complain about something they hadn't done right.

His mother kept her anger inside until her later years, but
the anger was obvious, nonetheless, and it permeated the
household. Even as a grown man, Dave's dealings with his
parents were not easy. In fact, they were painful and generally dreaded. His new sobriety seemed to be a threat to his
family. His dad couldn't accept that Dave couldn't have "even
one drink" with him anymore, and his comments bordered
on ridicule of Dave.

NEW HOPE

The one thing that had begun to change for Dave since following his friend to AA was that he had more hope now than
he had ever had before. Like most of us, he had arrived at the

door of Alcoholics Anonymous totally hopeless, and the sober men he came to know offered him their hope until he was able to experience it for himself. This is probably the most significant of all of the gifts we are given in the fellowship.

It matters not if hope comes from a specific sponsor or the whole group. We can recognize when others have hope, when others see the glass half full rather than half empty, and this appeals to us. This realization that there is another way of seeing the situations in our life is the beginning of the miracle that is, in fact, becoming our life. And Dave was actually on the path to a far better life than he had ever known with the help of his sponsor and AA. However, his anger was still a hindrance. The promise of serenity will continue to elude us if we let anger bar the door.

Dave "came by his anger honestly." He had grown up surrounded by it; he naturally began to imitate it. It's difficult to make another behavior choice when few possibilities for how to behave are modeled in our formative years. Dave was simply a chip off the old block. His dad's anger was so deeply rooted that Dave never figured out where it came from, but his mom's anger most likely came from being married to a man who never appreciated her and who never thought she was quite as good "as the stock" he had come from. No matter how hard she tried, her accomplishments failed to meet the test of perfection he expected from her and their children. Her anger became transformed into ridicule of others, not so different from the ridicule she and Dave suffered, and Dave was very much affected by this.

Anger can be all-consuming, and yet it can recede, seeming to disappear almost, and then suddenly resurface, even stronger than before. During Dave's recuperation from a stroke, he was freer of anger than he had been for his whole life. Looking back on it one might say that when his life went topsy-turvy, he grabbed hold of his Higher Power like never before. The result was a peacefulness that was unfamiliar to him and that he deeply appreciated.

Every detail of his life, for a period of time, made him grateful, he said. He was glad to be alive. He was glad he could speak, even though his ability to read was hindered, as was his ability to do the mathematical functions that were necessary to his profession. Nonetheless, he wore a smile, seemed filled with love for others, and felt grateful to the fellowship and to everyone who shared the fellowship with him.

Dave's brief experience with overwhelming gratitude, contrasted with the all-too-familiar anger, is not unusual in the life of the alcoholic. Whether we are in recovery or still in the throes of the addiction, we travel this well-worn path from one emotion to the other with frequency. Nevertheless, we are able to pass on the good that we have learned to others who look to us for counsel and hope. Dave was adept at passing it on. Just as he was able to learn from the old-timers who knew his story almost without his even having to tell it, he, too, could almost read the minds of his sponsees, and he knew the best antidote for their ailments.

In Dave's favor, he has always relied on sponsors since coming into the fellowship. Before then he had generally fought listening to the advice of others, assuming that there was a hidden agenda that he hadn't uncovered. Giving up his former suspiciousness has had big payoffs. He has made significant progress in every aspect of his life. He also has been able to encourage the same progress in many others.

A MUTUAL HEALING

Having a sponsor who was willing to listen for however long it took for Dave to share what was on his mind is what had the most impact on him, he said. He wasn't used to this in his family of origin or his first two marriages, and he had accumulated years of experiences that needed airing out. Andy, his first sponsor, was very gentle, a trait that Dave had never observed or experienced in his family of origin. Andy never passed judgment, he never even made many suggestions, but he listened intently and for as long as Dave needed to talk. He simply sat and listened. He smiled and nodded and said, "I understand." Dave felt from Andy the affirmation he had longed for all his life.

When Andy moved, it was necessary for Dave to get another sponsor. This new sponsor differed in many ways. He did the talking far more often than Dave did. He gave specifics and lots of directions for Dave to follow. And Dave did. Tom seemed to see that Dave was floundering. He saw it as his assignment to get Dave back on track. What's extremely important for our purposes here is to realize and even celebrate the differences in sponsors. As I have said earlier, there is no pamphlet that says sponsorship must be done in a specific way. However, an important trait is the sponsor's openness and willingness to let the inner voice of God direct him or her in what words should be offered as the "next best thing for the sponsee to do." Sponsorship is about availability, about listening, about reading the signs of what might be needed, and about strengthening one's own sobriety first and foremost. Sharing one's experience, strength, and hope is an antidote that could offer healing to what ails most of our society. It certainly heals the two who share the sponsorship experience.

One of the things Dave came to understand in his own recovery was his struggle with other people, places, and things. There is no better place to discover the ready and available help for dealing with the reality of all of these uncontrollables than through the Al-Anon program. Dave was one of the few alcoholics I spoke with who had added this dimension to his or her recovering life. It has been my supposition for nearly all of the years of my own recovery that Al-Anon would greatly enhance the individual recovery of any alcoholic. Alcoholics Anonymous keeps us sober, but Al-Anon teaches us how to serenely live in our many relationships. Even though anger continued to plague Dave's steps, he was sober, he was able to look at his behavior, and he was aware that without the fellowship he wouldn't be alive to share any of what he had learned.

Dave still doesn't trust many people outside of the walls of the fellowship. And he still has his own demons to confront. Perfectionism still haunts him, he says, as evidenced by his need for absolute order in his closets and dresser drawers. But he has learned to be more generous with the failure of others to be perfect. Perhaps this was passed on to him subliminally from Andy, his own favorite sponsor. Andy never pointed out Dave's many imperfections. He simply supported his efforts to try, again and again, to find peace in his life.

When I reflect on all Dave shared with me, I marvel at his continuous sobriety. The anger and sadness around his family of origin, the stroke and all its concomitant struggles, not to mention the unsuccessful marriages, could have pushed another alcoholic over the edge and into a pity pot big enough to make the allure of alcohol irresistible. But Dave kept doing what he had learned to do from those in the fellowship who knew best what to do. He doubled up on meetings, rather than falling away. He talked to his sponsor rather than isolating. And he prayed. Andy had impressed on Dave the importance of prayer in any form. Dave took his message to heart and relied on prayer every day. It mattered not that Andy was no longer physically present in Dave's life; his lifesaving advice was.

KEEP SHOWING UP

The presence of anger in our lives is commonplace among us alcoholics, sober or still drunk. Just because a person is struggling with the demon of anger doesn't mean he or she has no value as a sponsor, nor does it mean the still angry person just isn't listening well enough to his own sponsor. Anger is often a given in our lives. But it doesn't have to be eternal. It doesn't have to constantly control us. Nor does it have to be the only emotion we have. Most important, it doesn't have to keep us from giving away the parts of the program that have worked well in our lives.

Dave proves this because he keeps showing up and giving away what he knows to be true. I know, from sitting in meetings with him over the years, that he speaks the truth, no matter how flawed it makes him look. That's the bottom line to continuous recovery. We must be humble and honest enough to share our deepest thoughts and fears, regardless of how we think they make us look, if we expect to stay sober. In fact, it's the only way we can stay sober!

Dave's life is far from perfect. He is still struggling with anger and some fear, but he has not veered from this fellowship since he first made his commitment to it approximately twenty-five years ago. What he has said to me many times is that he is grateful, that he will keep giving it away, that he knows he is where he needs to be, and that God isn't done offering him lessons. I know that the same is true for you. Likewise for me.

TRANSFORMATION

One of the most effective things a sponsor can do, for himself and the newcomer, is to tell the truth. We cannot help or be helped if we pretend life has been other than what it actually was. Being told that simply telling the truth is the way to sponsor another person helps us realize that each of us is capable of sponsorship. Over the years I have heard from many people, "Oh, I don't know how to be a sponsor." My response is, "You know your story, don't you?" That's what sponsorship is about. Every time you tell how it worked for you, you strengthen your awareness of how far you have come so that you won't be tempted to *go back there* ever again.

I have come to believe that alcoholics are the luckiest people alive. Because we need to talk to one another to stay sober, we have the opportunity to heal much more in ourselves than just the alcoholism. We are not unique individuals, really. Every person alive suffers from imagined or real inadequacies. But not every person alive has the impetus we each have to talk about these inadequacies and thus move on with our lives. By talking and listening, we can find relief, at the very least, and ultimately we will be healed. I don't mean to imply "cured" when I say "healed," but I do think our minds can heal: they can be at peace, they can be filled with trust and love, and nothing about our everyday circumstances will ever look the same again. For no other malady can one be quite as certain that this will be the outcome.

I would like to suggest that one of the most important results of involvement in the fellowship, which also means taking on the role of sponsorship, is that our hearts are changed. I really can't say for certain just how or when this phenomenon occurs, but it does. After much rumination about this, I have concluded that the process that results in this change is our willingness to foster and then participate in open, honest communication. I am convinced that we don't listen just through our ears. Our hearts can hear things that our ears miss, and when we engage them as well as the ears, they soften just a bit on every occasion. Softened hearts are what really influence the world about us. Not only are the men and women in recovery affected by the changes that occur in our hearts, but every person and every situation we encounter wears the mark of a heart that has been changed.

I have heard some people in the fellowship say that those of us who are lucky enough to "have been called" to this program are the *way-showers* of the future to all the rest of humanity. I have no idea if that's true, but we have been given an opportunity to learn how to interact in loving ways with total strangers. When any person, anywhere, feels the hand of love present and extended, he or she is changed forever. You and I are part of this chain of change.

As I've mentioned before, and it bears repeating, we need focus on principles, not personalities. At first I had no idea what my sponsor meant when she asked this. I was sure I was more focused on personalities, as a matter of fact. Some individuals had very dominant ones, naturally, but what I eventually realized was that some who caught my attention talked a talk they didn't very adeptly walk. This was my sponsor's real message. "See what they do, not just what they say."

Another thing I learned from this axiom about principles versus personalities was that the personalities who bugged me often had the most to teach me in the way of a program principle. For instance, there was a man in one of the groups I went to in the early days who droned on and on at every meeting. I often felt like speaking for the whole group and telling him to shut up, certain that the group would have not only approved but applauded my effort. Fortunately I didn't do that. I came to understand that they wouldn't have approved at all. What my silence helped me to see eventually was that I had a lot to learn about my own intolerance, my own impatience, and my own need to be the center of attention.

I also eventually grew to like the man who seemed to talk too much, and I was able to realize that he had a lot of wisdom. I also finally noticed that the other group members didn't appear at all bothered by his contributions at a meeting. The problem was clearly mine, not his or anyone else's in the group.

A DAILY INVENTORY

Perhaps one of the greatest gifts of the fellowship and having a sponsor is that we come to understand through all that we hear that *we are the problem,* no one else. How much we all long to blame another individual for whatever ails us. But a good sponsor and every person at any meeting who is really trying to recover will always say the problem isn't *out there.* It's *in here,* as they point to themselves. The "in here" can best be understood through diligently doing an inventory.

Most sponsors will suggest doing an inventory on a daily basis. It's the best way to keep the personal slate clean, and the best way to keep feelings from cluttering up your mind. When feelings linger, they will begin to clutter up your actions, too. Keep it simple. Before going to bed at night, note what is going through your mind. Note what has been bothering you throughout the day. Jot these things down but also be vigilant about noting what you felt good about along with what you wish you had not said or done. If we stay on top of a simple inventory of this kind, our imperfect behavior won't escalate into actions that shame us for months to come, or worse, actions that might trigger a relapse. It is really so simple to keep our lives in check, and sponsors are available to help us every step of the way.

There are many kinds of sponsors. There are those we specifically invite to help us understand the fine points of the program. These are the ones who generally make sure we are doing the Steps, attending meetings, and developing a relationship with a Higher Power to the best of our ability. They insist that we call them often or perhaps they will call us. They feel perfectly justified in getting on our case if we are falling down as far as meetings, reading, or praying are concerned. Many of us would not have stayed sober had it not been for the intense attention we got from a sponsor.

Equally important are the sponsors who wander in and through our lives, sharing a thought or two that lingers after they have gone. This thought may well guide us to take a new path or perhaps pursue a new goal. Many times this person will literally save a life, as was the case for me.

One of the ways my own sponsor helped me when I first came into the fellowship was to explain, by her own example, the meaning behind the words in the Steps. I was embarrassed to admit in group that I couldn't understand what they meant, and what "unmanageability" meant escaped me entirely.

My sponsor educated me through using her own missteps as the examples for clarity. In this way I was able to see that she, too, had been as confused as I was when she first got sober. I could also see that she was no longer embarrassed to reveal her earlier ignorance about the meaning behind the words. This was great modeling for someone like me. I hated to let others know that I was in the dark about a particular idea. My fear of how they might judge me was so great. That she no longer had this fear gave me hope in a subtle way.

Every story I have shared with you thus far has had evidence of at least one person who unexpectedly came along at just the right time to change the storyteller's life. Remember the friend who took Dave to his first AA meeting. Dave had not sought his help, nor did Dave know his friend was in AA. But he showed up, anyway, at just the right time, and he stayed in Dave's life. He is still in Dave's life, in fact.

Innumerable "sponsors" entered the next woman's life just by being present at the many meetings she wandered into before she was ready to actually hear what any one of them said. The truth of the matter is, it doesn't matter that she was present but didn't hear what was being shared. She heard their messages when the time was right for her to hear them. And more important, each of the individuals sharing a message with Tina was hearing a message he or she needed to hear repeated anyway. That's one of the biggest pluses of sponsorship. The sponsee doesn't have to listen, he or she doesn't have to follow the suggestion, or even get or stay sober. The messenger is the one who is truly helped by the message. This was demonstrated for us through "the coming together" of Bill W. and Dr. Bob. If we can remember this, we all will have greater clarity about why we should offer our services as sponsors, and if we are sponsees, we will be much less fearful about making the call to our sponsor and asking for help. Every call that a sponsee makes to a sponsor gives that sponsor another reason for staying sober one more day.

THIRTEEN

LEAVE YOUR CAMPSITE
BETTER THAN YOU FOUND IT

TINA'S STORY

Tina could well be considered a hard case. By age twelve she was buying and smoking cigarettes on a regular basis, and soon after she was drinking beer, which helped to block out the verbal and emotional abuse that her dad, an active alcoholic, inflicted on her at home. But no doubt, even if he had not been abusive, Tina would have been drinking. From her very first drink on, she was entranced by the effects of alcohol. The instability at home was a good excuse for her deviant behavior but probably not a necessary one.

Her parents split up when she was twelve, and she lived with her mom for the first year. Because she was hanging out with a rough crowd, she eventually chose to live with her dad for a while. She had more freedom under his roof. By age thirteen, unbeknownst to her dad, who was usually out all night, she, too, was staying out all night, drinking and drugging. Tina hated school and the demands placed on her. Her regimen of speed, LSD, PCP, angel dust, and the ever-present alcohol made quitting school at age sixteen almost a given.

Even though she watched friends experience "brain melts" from their reckless use of heavy street drugs, Tina's own behavior changed very little. Like every addict, she felt invincible. She moved back in with her mom after the brief stint with her dad, but was kicked out after a short time as the result of her drug use and her incorrigibility. Being homeless posed no problem in her mind. She knew she could always move in with her boyfriend. And she did.

She enrolled in beauty school, and she and her boyfriend bought a trailer. She didn't consider that her life would or should ever be much different. Not until she went to a family program as part of her dad's failed treatment for alcoholism did she begin to consider that she, too, might be alcoholic. But it mattered little to her at the time. So what? Tina was doing what she wanted to do.

She went to work as a beautician, left her boyfriend, moved in with girlfriends, and soon began stealing from her employer to support her drug habit and her lifestyle. By age eighteen she "had graduated" to working as a bartender, dealing drugs, and doing cocaine. Jobs were dispensable; drugs weren't. Her mother never gave up on her and tried to keep her connected to the family. She kept inviting her to "come home, come to grandma's, join us for the holidays," and so on, but Tina maintained her distance, while all the time expecting, at an almost unconscious level, that someone would eventually intervene, as had happened to her dad.

Tina finally had no place else to go but her mom's home, since her housemates had kicked her out. Her paranoia was escalating, as was her agoraphobia. Finally she went to a psychologist to deal with her deteriorating mental and emotional condition, and he suggested she go to treatment. This certainly made sense. By now, it only took two drinks to put her in a blackout.

She could no longer drive; she had become terrified of everything, even the effects of cocaine. But inpatient treatment was too risky, she thought. Outpatient treatment was the only option that would let her keep tabs on her new boyfriend. It won't surprise you to learn that she didn't stay sober, not even for a few days. In fact, nothing changed. She resumed exactly where she had left off, hanging out with her using buddies, thinking very little about what she wanted for her future.

A TASTE OF THE FELLOWSHIP

Tina did, in time, end up in Alcoholics Anonymous. She wasn't even clear in her mind, when she shared her story with me, how coming to AA the first time actually happened. But some angel in disguise led her our way and she got a taste of what the fellowship had to offer. She didn't stick around long the first time, but as was true for so many of us, once introduced to the fellowship, drinking was never the same for her again.

Not long after her introduction to AA, she met the man who was to become her husband, and although he wasn't a "program guy," he was a good and decent man, a far different kind of person than the men she had gravitated to before. She still considers his interest in her at that time a significant event in her life. She began to see healthier possibilities for how life might be lived than the possibilities she had grown accustomed to.

However, she wasn't yet finished with her using life, either. She relapsed a number of times, but one relapse, in particular, was terrifying; we might call it her key turning point. After being sober a few months, Tina woke up in a strange apartment and didn't know where she was, what day it was, how she got there, or with whom. She had no idea in which direction to head when she discovered her car down the street from the apartment. Nothing was familiar about the street names, the houses, the scenery. For the first time she was filled with a fear that truly haunted her. She didn't want this life or these experiences anymore. She returned to the fellowship with a new resolve.

Every one of us gets to recovery the only way we can. Some never have to go back out and try using again, while others of us do, repeatedly. The lucky ones make it back to the program. Since that return more than a dozen years ago, Tina has not wandered. But getting the program took a while. Fortunately for many of us, the program will finally "get us" if we just stick around. This was true for Tina. She didn't immediately get a sponsor. She didn't go to many meetings at first. She was haphazard about working the Steps, but she didn't drink. And when she went to meetings, she listened. She also became acutely aware of the peace some people had in her home group. She knew she wanted to share in that peace. They told her to keep coming back and to stay willing to listen. She did, and then, ever so slowly, life began to change in miraculous ways.

Tina still can't believe all of the changes that have occurred in her life. First of all, she got her GED and then enrolled in college. She earned a bachelor's degree and maintained a 3.5 grade point average. The girl who had hated school discovered just how smart she really was. She married the good man she had met a couple of years before, and he was supportive of her sober life. Next, she began working as a professional in an occupation that was related to her ongoing sobriety. This offered her the chance every day to tell others how to live the program that was, in fact, saving her life, too.

THE PAYOFF OF STICKING AROUND

Tina was and still is the angel in disguise for many individuals, and she recognizes that many angels have been on her path all along. Every person at any meeting is an angel in disguise, in the final analysis. We have been sent on a mission, I believe. Some of us hear the call, while others turn a deaf ear, but nonetheless, it is by design that we finally gather together.

Tina shared with me some recollections she had of people who just seemed to be there when she needed the extra help. For instance, the woman she had never seen before who walked up to her at a meeting just when she was considering bolting for the door in fear. Or the time she had the opportunity to help a newcomer when she was feeling particularly down herself. Sharing with Gillian her own fears and desire to run on occasion gave Tina a reason to stick around. She wanted to show Gillian that there were payoffs for sticking around. Both she and Gillian profited from this experience.

I knew exactly how she felt about these chance experiences or opportunities to talk with someone. My recollection about Pat's visit to me is never far from my memory. At the time it is happening, we seldom appreciate the fullness of the miracle. In retrospect, we will see how our perspective, our understanding, in fact our entire life actually changed as the result of one person connecting with us at a distinctly crucial time. We can be grateful, only then, that we had become willing to put ourselves in the flow and listen. Tina became a great listener.

Tina also became a prizewinning horsewoman, a sport she had dropped many years earlier before her drug use took over her life. Riding and showing horses had been her love from the time she was a young girl, but Tina had had neither the time, the energy, nor the money to pursue the activities of the horse world while in the throes of her addiction. Now she needed these activities as a healthy focus for her life. Her friends were glad for her return and she had the opportunity in this setting to share with other young people in the sport some of what she had learned on her own "road to destruction." It was now her turn to give away what she was learning about finding the peaceful life, and she was a great purveyor of *this truth* that she was discovering for herself.

We are in process, always. We learn and then we share and then we learn some more. This was and is true for Tina. It was and is true for you and me, too. Tina's process for learning has brought her full circle to the spiritual life she left behind so many years before. She had thought of prayer as "religion" as a child, and as a young adult and she wanted nothing to do with it. Now she was able to see that she needed and wanted God in her life for direction and comfort. God had always been there, she knew, but she had not felt the desire to acknowledge him. In fact, she was repulsed by the thought of acknowledging him. Now she appreciated the opportunities to acknowledge God, and the peace began to come.

TRUSTING AND WAITING

Tina's learning curve has now included the celebration of relationships, too. Not unlike most of us, Tina had been afraid of relationships. None of hers had nurtured her, outside of those with her mother and grandparents. Even when she entered the rooms of the fellowship, she was afraid of the offering of friendship from individuals at first. What would be asked of her in return, she wondered? She has come to understand that in these rooms all that is asked in return is honesty, a willingness to listen, and a desire to pass on to others what one has learned. This Tina became willing to do.

Most important, Tina became willing to talk to her sponsor about the secrets in her life that were keeping her stuck. She had many. The sponsor's words, in return, gave her hope and the impetus she needed to simply continue moving forward, in a mostly straight line. What we all come to realize, if we are willing to remember the many instances from the past, is that these seemingly happenstance messages spoken to us by particular individuals at specific times are messages from God. They do give us the comfort and the hope we need. We learn in these rooms and from our sponsors that God is never too busy to notice exactly what we need. God will make the direction we need known to us. Our assignment is to listen for it and then heed it.

Tina remembers with gratitude when she first heard these words from her sponsor: "You are enough. You are where you need to be. Wait and the answer will come." She was distraught at the time—restless and wondering if she was going in the right direction. She wondered if she really was where she needed to be, in the marriage that was right for her, doing the work that was truly hers to do. She was antsy to move on, a feeling familiar to her from her using days. Back then, she tended to quickly move on. Another boyfriend, a different drug, a different combination of drugs, perhaps. Anything to "mix it up a little" was what she always sought when feeling bored.

Tina's sponsor never left her side, in a way. Though not physically always with her, her words seemed to hang in the air, and Tina clung to them as if they were a life raft. They held her up when her own thoughts wanted to pull her down. Like a voice from the heavens, her sponsor's words kept reminding her, "You don't have to know where you are

going. It's a journey, and there is peace in not knowing, but
simply trusting and waiting." Tina did learn to trust and wait,
and she became a believer in perhaps her sponsor's most
important message: "God's will is loving thought. Nothing
more." This brought her profound relief and gratitude. Most
of us have wrung our hands and searched our minds seeking
to know God's will. Is it this pathway or that? Are we to do
this work or go back to school? Should we stay in this relationship or move on? The questions that plague us, particularly in early recovery, can paralyze us. Some drink again
because of them. And some who do, never return.

Tina's occasional ennui, though a common characteristic
among recovering men and women, was greatly soothed by
the information that God's will was simply to be loving toward others. She knew she could do this at least some of the
time. She couldn't quickly and easily decide whether she
needed to switch jobs or marriages or friends, but she could
decide that in any particular moment she could offer love to
the specific person in her presence. This was doable! What
had once been true for Tina is what is true for many of us on
occasion. We resist this offering of love. Instead, we hold
back, waiting for the other person to make the first move. Or
when they do, we turn our backs. It's not so easy to love
everyone on our path, every time, is it?

I am reminded again of the wonderful story about the
Dalai Lama that I mentioned earlier in this book. If we can't
offer love in return, or if we can't be the initiator of the offering of love, we can at least refrain from hurting the person
on our path. He or she is there by design, and God is in
charge of the appointment. Tina was learning this and wanting desperately to celebrate it, but she feared she was still
a "con artist" at heart. Her expression of love was often ma-
nipulative, she thought. She sometimes referred to herself as
a "recovering liar."

Many of us might well belong in that category along with Tina. How recently did you tell a simple little lie to make yourself appear better than you are? Even as sober men and women, even in long-term sobriety, we can fall into the trap of wanting to improve our image, and the quickest way to get there is by stretching the truth about us, just a little bit. But that little bit is still a lie. Let's not forget it. The lies can add up to the shame that takes us back out, a place not one of us wants to go. "Back out" is certainly not a place Tina wants to go again, which is why she in all seriousness refers to herself as a recovering liar. Her honesty about this will save her from a relapse.

THE MAIN THING: SPONSORSHIP

Tina offers a number of suggestions to newcomers based on her personal experiences, which I want to share with you because of the wisdom of her suggestions. She says, "Sponsorship is important. In fact, it's the main thing. Working with another person is what makes recovery work. Surrendering is the significant turning point when entering the program." And the easiest way to surrender, Tina and many others have learned, is with the help of a sponsor. Our resistance to getting well will melt away when we allow ourselves to be heard, really heard, and thus helped by one who has walked in our shoes.

It bears repeating: the sponsee is not the only person who is helped by sponsorship. In fact, the sponsor may even be helped more than the sponsee. Without the newcomers in our midst, how many of us would still be sober?

Although Tina struggled to get to our fellowship, she is now aware that she was getting important messages all of her life. One that came to her from an unlikely source and that has remained with her for years because of its profundity is

"Leave your campsite better than you found it." This homily, posted at a favorite camping spot, speaks to us from many perspectives. Leave the meeting better than you found it. Leave the program better than you found it. Leave the fellowship better than you found it. Leave your sponsor better than you found him or her. Leave your spouse, your friend, your child, your employer, your employee, your parents, your neighbors better than you found them. In other words, bring your best self to every situation and each experience and it will be elevated to the benefit of all concerned.

Tina lived on life's fast track for so many years. Even well into recovery she pines for the fast track occasionally. A counselor once told her she "loved shiny things." That was his way of letting her know she lived on the slippery edge too much of the time. She recognizes this and doesn't want to fall over the edge. Nor does she really want to surrender the excitement that the edge offers. One key line that rings in her ears when she gets too close to the edge is a definition a friend offered her: "Serenity is that one moment when you put someone else's needs before your own." It's not easy to stay on the edge if we are thinking of someone else's well-being. And when we are on the edge, *there is no serenity.*

Tina sees herself as a slow learner. On the other hand, based on my interviews with her, I would say she has learned well and completely that which has given her a solid foundation. She is eager to pass on to others what has worked in her life. She has continued to make steady progress in her marriage, her profession, and in the most personal aspects of her life. Her motto is "I am of service," and she demonstrates this every day on the job and with newcomers. Tina is the embodiment of the belief that many of us share: AA is the way back to life, to family, to responsibilities.

Tina left me with many specific thoughts she has gathered

from others, and since we all believe that to continue to grow, each of us must pass on to others what we have learned, I want to share a few more of these thoughts with you. After all, my sobriety continues to be the most important aspect of my life, as well. From Tina and her many angels in disguise come these words: "Life isn't happening to me. I am making it what it is. Perception is the key. I am here to be joyful but also to discover my purpose, my role. We can grow from the bad and the good. Strength can come from anywhere. I tip my hat to strength. I don't have to figure out anything."

It was pure joy talking with and listening to Tina. Though young, she expresses a wisdom that will usher significant awarenesses into the hearts of many others for years to come. We are all the recipients of this. And that's the miracle of this way of life.

THE ENORMITY OF FEAR

How was it that the founders of AA understood so clearly that the key to sustained sobriety was through the channel of communication with one another? Surely they had grown up in families where secrets were sacred. They didn't learn the importance of sharing one's inner turmoil from English or history books, the media, or the psychology books popular then. Nor did they have personal experience with support groups, which foster the idea of sharing our fears and struggles. Yet they "fathered" just such a system for the rest of us. Surely the hand of a Greater Being was involved.

Fear is no doubt one of the foremost problems for any member of our universal society, but it is the paramount problem for the newcomer to Alcoholics Anonymous. Fear continues to be a leading problem for many recovering people even though they have been able to maintain their sobriety.

Let's remember that fear was the impetus that sent Bill W. to Dr. Bob's bedside more than sixty-five years ago.

In that particular case, fear kept Bill sober for another day. But when we look at this situation a little more closely, we would have to say that what actually kept Bill sober was the fact that he sought out another suffering soul to share his story with. While it's true that he desperately wanted a drink and was afraid he would weaken and order one if he didn't do something drastic to prevent it, the talking he did is what actually kept him sober, not the fear. This is an important distinction. Fear is normal. We can't escape it. But every one of us in Alcoholics Anonymous has a prescription for treating fear.

I have made many pronouncements about sponsorship throughout this book. I have said it's mandatory if one wants to heal the pain and the disease of alcoholism. I have advocated same-sex sponsorship as the best kind, at least in early recovery. I have suggested that a sponsor needs a sponsee just as much as a sponsee needs a sponsor. I have said that one has to give away to others what one has received in order to keep it, and sponsorship is the best avenue for doing this.

Sponsorship is not the same thing as friendship, and, in fact, being a "friend" is not necessary for the sponsor to be an effective sponsor. Some old-timers would even suggest that your sponsor isn't your friend and shouldn't be your friend. I personally don't go that far, but friendship can get in the way of speaking the very truth a sponsee needs to hear at a particular time. It's crucial that a sponsor feel free to pass on what has worked for her even if the words are not welcome to the sponsee. This is not always easy if the sponsee is also a bosom buddy.

There is no rule book about what a sponsor must do in his or her role with a sponsee, and individual sponsors generally have their own interpretation of how to pass on the program to someone new. Often, they will pass on what they have learned in a manner similar to how the information was passed on to them, particularly if they feel their current sobriety is the direct result of that particular method.

Sponsoring a person who has longer sobriety but who is still struggling may well be done in a different manner. Some may need a "tough love" approach while others need a gentler hand. However, there are some specifics that all serious sponsors adhere to. Just as I noted in the story about Tina and her sponsor, the sponsor shares first and foremost what has effectively worked for her. She emphasizes the importance of working the Steps, attending numerous meetings every week, making telephone calls to others in the fellowship on a regular basis, and doing service work from the onset of this journey.

IT'S OKAY TO SAY NO

Sponsors have agreed to make themselves available to listen and offer guidance to the newcomer, or to the old-timer in search of a new sponsor, by the very fact that they said yes when asked to be a sponsor. However, it is okay to say no when asked to be a sponsor, too. Not every request for sponsorship needs to be agreed to. It's important that each person in our fellowship do what he or she needs to do for recovery, and stretching oneself too thin by being available to too many people helps no one, in the final analysis.

It's terribly important for newcomers to understand the purpose of sponsorship. It's also important that they know that every person in the fellowship feared making that first call or asking that first person to be a sponsor. We are all very much alike. Generally, what one person fears, we all fear.

That's one of the reasons we understand each other so well. It's also the reason we can often recognize what each other needs.

Sponsorship is the perfect avenue for people like us. What we needed from others is what we can now offer to others. Tina, like all of the storytellers, shared with me how crucial a particular bit of information was or a specific instance when someone called by phone or entered the room at the exact right time with a lifesaving message. A coincidence? We think not. The relief that is felt, through and through, when a message of hope is delivered and then heard can't be explained to one who hasn't experienced it. Those of us who have will always treasure it, though, and understand it as the grace of God. Isn't it awesome to look around our fellowship on a regular basis and reflect on the number of instances that grace has occurred? For every person present, we can no doubt count at least one time.

I was profoundly moved by the experiences I had with each storyteller, particularly as I ruminated on the miraculous journey each had made to our fellowship and the evidence of grace in each person's life. But the next storyteller clearly appeared to be on the road to destruction. Her journey to us was similar to Tina's in many respects. It was full of danger, recklessness, and living on the edge. Her very survival amazes me. And yet I know, as do you, that she was destined to survive or she wouldn't have. It is not by accident that we finally get here. It's by divine appointment, and if we are meant to be here, we will not have been able to avoid it or escape it. Never doubt that this has been true for you, too. If you are reading this now, you were selected.

FOURTEEN

TO BE PART OF GOD

ROBYN'S STORY

The allure of cigarettes captured Robyn at age eleven, just as it had captured Tina. It is a gateway drug, without a doubt. Not long after the cigarettes claimed her, she turned to other drugs for the simple thrill and hope of being part of the crowd. Not surprisingly, doing drugs with this crowd gave her the illusion of belonging. Robyn felt the connection she craved when they shared their speed, their pot, and their alcohol with her.

How Robyn ended up on this road is a bit more of a mystery than had been true for Tina. In Tina's case, the addiction was a natural progression in her family of origin. A dysfunctional family, an alcoholic dad, and the emotional abuse all quickly combined to make the escape into alcohol and drugs understandable. Robyn, on the other hand, was not emotionally abused. Her parents were not alcoholics. They were loving, gentle, supportive, and concerned. They were high achievers in their personal lives and were certain Robyn would follow suit. She was exceedingly bright. But she was also easily bored, an unfortunate combination. The attraction to drugs as a way out of the boredom is a natural step for some. Robyn fit this profile.

Her academic achievements were outstanding. She skipped two grades in school. She was a sure superstar until she experienced the physical and emotional transformation that chemicals gave her. From that moment on, she was willing to give up everything for the effects of the drugs. She felt some sadness that she could no longer concentrate, but that didn't make her question her new path. The drugs were just too good. They quickly claimed her as a prisoner, and she willingly surrendered. When she wasn't under their influence, she isolated herself. Either way, she no longer connected with her family. She was the "tornado" in their home, wreaking havoc at every turn, and they were confused by the ambush.

Robyn describes herself as a high-maintenance child. She was emotional, creative, bright, and uncontrollable. She clearly was marked for academic and personal success and she was blowing it. She didn't care. The drugs had already begun to do her thinking for her. She could give up everything for them and not look back. Fortunately her parents had other plans for Robyn. They put her in treatment the first time when she was fifteen. She didn't care, one way or the other, what they did about her life. She felt nothing, but she was sure abstinence wasn't the path for her, not yet anyway. The first speaker she heard in treatment convinced her of this. Sobriety looked like a dead end and she wasn't ready for it.

She proved this by walking out of treatment early, but she didn't go home, not right away. She slept on the streets for a while. She realized that something was terribly wrong and that she was in trouble. She feared insanity because of her lack of clarity, but she couldn't make a different choice. With no place to go, she returned home eventually and even escaped into her studies for a while. Sober, but not happy, she let school absorb her attention for a few months. She studied for hours at a time, around the clock. It absolutely consumed her, just as drugs had, and she excelled in her studies. Then one day she walked out of the house and used again. With no forethought, she simply resumed where she had left off as a druggie.

This was a pattern that was to be repeated many times in Robyn's life, much to the confusion of her parents. They had always been supportive in all of the right ways. They loved her unconditionally and she knew it. Nothing about her home life was pushing her in this deviant direction. Yet, she walked away from her family, time and again. The insanity of Robyn's disease was far more powerful than the love of her family.

THE INSANITY OF THE DISEASE

Again Robyn went to treatment. With a firm resolve this time, she entered the program and finished it. Her first day out of treatment she was using again. She emphatically announced to others, "I have decided to drink again." The insanity of the disease is certainly apparent in this decision. She looks back on this behavior and shakes her head, as confused by it now as her parents were then.

Robyn's next treatment experience was shared with her grandmother. The family had never made a big issue of her grandmother's alcoholism, and the genetic connection was never discussed. It certainly was there, nonetheless. The value of sharing this experience with her grandmother was that Robyn could see where she was headed if she didn't do something about her own addiction. Her grandmother was the mirror that Robyn needed. She even said to herself, "I will be my grandmother someday unless something changes." But the time still wasn't quite right. One of the sad corollaries of Robyn's story is that her grandmother was never to find sobriety.

Robyn is aware today that her main stumbling block to recovery was her refusal to do what was suggested to her. Get
a sponsor? No way! Go to meetings! Are you kidding? She
didn't consider herself a group person. She was too smart for
that. Her intellect got in her way. She couldn't listen because
she was so busy thinking, and her thoughts carried her right
back out to her using friends, again and again. Relapsing was
her pattern and she saw no reason to change it. She didn't
seem to care, or perhaps she didn't recognize the danger in
her many trips back out. At this point she seemed to assume
that the revolving door in and out of sobriety was normal and
that it would always open and close and open again.

Before Robyn's last treatment, the hallucinations that had
begun much earlier in her journey had escalated to a high
pitch. Her drinking was suicidal. At times she couldn't physically stand up, so she crawled. She began to suspect that her
time was running out. Fortunately her younger brother came
to her rescue. With hope now fully gone, she finally surrendered. Nearly fifteen years after her first treatment, which
was followed by numerous subsequent treatments, Robyn
reluctantly said, "I am ready." She was resigned simply because everything else had failed. She was highly intelligent
but she hadn't been smart enough to continue this way of life
and stay alive. And she knew it. Her last treatment finally got
her attention.

A KINDRED SOUL

The counselor-in-training assigned to Robyn is the person
who really got her attention. She was smart, unflappable, and
streetwise. Robyn's actions, both before and during treatment, were nothing new to Heidi. She had seen it all and
had done it all herself. The synchronicity of Robyn's being in

treatment at the same time that Heidi was in training is one of the marvelous miracles God had in store for Robyn. We seldom appreciate the miracles as they are occurring. This was true for Robyn, but by the time we talked, she had realized quite fully the impact that Heidi had had on her treatment, her self-awareness, her nascent understanding of God, and her desire to have a different life.

Why was it that Robyn could hear Heidi when she couldn't hear others carrying the same message earlier? Was it because they were close in age and had traveled similar paths? Perhaps. But most likely it's no more complicated than that the time was finally right for Robyn. There is seldom a mysterious explanation to why something eventually makes sense. It just does. We are simply in an open frame of mind. The teacher is present, the student is ready. The seed for change is planted, the seed grows.

Robyn's first actual awareness that something was different this time was an experience she had when on a walking assignment given to her by the counselor. She was told to "find God" and write about her discovery. She walked through the woods on the grounds of the treatment center in search of God. What does God look like? Where is he now? Heidi gave no explicit directions. She simply said, "You have to have a God in your life. Now go find him." With no specific directions to follow, she felt terrified. She was used to a script for doing an assignment. She began to cry. She felt hopeless. She kept saying to herself, "I can't do this. I wish I were different. I wish I could see the beauty all around me."

Even though she felt unsure of herself during her walk and had no idea what to write, she began to let the words in her mind write themselves. "There are things that are good and things that are bad. If you want to be a part of God, you have to be good." She had no idea where the words came from.

She had not had this thought before she wrote it, not that she remembered. It was simply there in her mind and it ended up on her paper. Proud to have written the word "God" on her paper, she got up from the bench on the path in the woods to return to her unit, feeling that she had finished the assignment to the best of her ability. In the next moment an owl flew down the path directly toward her and landed at her feet. Instantly she saw and knew the power of God. From that moment on, nothing looked or felt the same. She feared her counselor might call her experience "a bunch of crap," but she knew something miraculous had happened in that moment when she and the owl stared at one another. She felt excitement for the first time in years.

Her remaining time in treatment stabilized her. She now desired what had never beckoned to her before. She wanted sobriety; she wanted to know God; she wanted to live sanely and fully. And she wanted healthy relationships, whatever those were. After treatment she went to live in a halfway house, got involved in Alcoholics Anonymous for the first time, and found her first sponsor. Never before when advised to get a sponsor had Robyn even considered it. This time she wouldn't have dared to resist the suggestion.

NEW SKILLS, NEW KNOWLEDGE

Robyn's first sponsor taught her things she didn't even realize she didn't know—for instance, how to begin appreciating the contributions of others and even how to relate to others on the simplest of levels. Robyn had been either an isolate or running with a pack who never listened for so long that she didn't realize that her social abilities were limited. Relating one to one was even harder than mixing in a group. Hiding out in her drugs or in her studies had taken a much bigger toll on Robyn's skills than she had imagined.

Evelyn was truly a godsend. Their daily discussions taught Robyn how to share feelings and thoughts, how to listen, and how to be truthful. They gave Robyn the courage to be absolutely honest and even secure in that honesty, a skill she had never acquired or sought before sobriety. After so many treatments, so many failed attempts at staying sober, the relationship between Robyn and her mother had become strained. It bordered on being volatile over the tiniest issues. Evelyn was a perfect person for Robyn to practice new behavior with, behavior that she wanted to show her mom. She was aware that Evelyn could say exactly the same things to her that her mother might have said, but she felt no need to react to Evelyn. Why was this the case? Did it have to be this way? Robyn wanted her part in the relationship with her mother to change, finally, and she worked to make that happen.

For the first eight years of Robyn's sobriety, she and Evelyn remained close. Robyn had a lot of work to do, and Evelyn was sent to help her do it. Robyn doesn't doubt this at all. Neither do I. The people carrying the traits we need to learn about will wander into our lives. We may refuse to acknowledge them at first, but they will return, again and again, if not in their initial form, then in the form of another person who shares those traits.

The journey is about learning that which we came here to learn. The opportunities for learning the lessons we need will not quit presenting themselves until we have addressed them, a fact we can be grateful for, because it means we don't have to learn it all perfectly the first time the opportunity presents itself.

Robyn married after a few years in the fellowship, to a man

who shared her recovery path. Together they created the joy of Robyn's life, a little boy whom she describes as the "best work" of their partnership. Even though the marriage didn't survive, the friendship did, as did the commitment to their son and to their individual recoveries.

Robyn clearly wants distance from a past that was so destructive to her and to her relationships. And just as clearly she knows that in the present she wants to be a good parent, a good daughter, a good role model for others in the program, a good sponsor, a good member of the fellowship, a good example of service work, a good woman, and a great example of one who "walks with God."

Robyn says that without Heidi as a counselor and the owl she faced on the path in the woods, she is not sure how her life might have unfolded. In concert, the two experiences helped her turn a crucial corner. It is important that we each look back on our specific experiences and acknowledge the hand of God that was there in each one. Not only is this important for our humility, it's important for our peace of mind. It is the one act that can convince us when we are wavering that we will not be forgotten in the future, just as we were never forgotten in the past.

A NEW SPONSOR

Robyn learned from Heidi, from Evelyn, from all of her home group friends, from her husband, and from her son that life is good and full of promise. She is still learning these things. She also learned that after eight years utilizing Evelyn's guidance, it was time to seek a new sponsor. Why does a person ever need to switch sponsors? It's generally not because of a serious problem. Most likely the reason is similar to Robyn's. She and Evelyn had become so enmeshed after eight years of intimately working together that Robyn couldn't hear Evelyn's suggestions clearly anymore. She lost track of which words were Evelyn's and which were her own. To recognize this and be willing to say a change is needed isn't always easy. It can be as difficult to "fire a sponsor" as it is to ask someone to be your sponsor the first time. But it is also true that both parties generally recognize a change is needed, and feelings are seldom hurt.

Robyn's new sponsor is helping her strengthen her spiritual ties. Robyn is reading the Big Book again and crying while reading every page. She says it's as though she is hearing the miracle of the lives saved from a heightened awareness. She realizes without a doubt that her current sponsor is the person she has been getting ready for. Although many times in more than ten years of recovery she has been moved to acknowledge God's role in her life, she has clearly been more "intellectual, more cerebral" than spiritual in her acceptance of the fellowship, her individual recovery, and the changes in her life. With Joy's guidance she is beginning to celebrate the lighter, softer side of her spiritual nature. She is consciously choosing to focus on the moment and be grateful for it and for the presence of God in it.

She is also consciously choosing to let others be who they are. She is learning that who they are is actually who she needs them to be in order to learn what she has come here to learn. This statement is as true for you and me as it is for Robyn. When we let others be who they really are, we change. And that's the key to healthy recovery. A line from another book I love by Helen Schucman is this: "Look not to change the world but to change your mind about the world." This we can do. It takes persistence and willingness, and we are endowed with those characteristics if we are sharing this path of recovery.

Robyn is learning so many things in this second decade of her recovery. The exciting thing for every one of us is that *school is in session* for our whole lives if we have the desire to continue educating ourselves. Some of us will have that desire. Some won't. But those of us who do have a task ahead of us. We are the way-showers for others. We are appointed to carry the message that life is filled with promise, with miracles, with hope, and with the awareness that a Higher Presence is available to carry your burden whenever you want to lay it aside.

Robyn is carrying her message every day. She is celebrating that we are "meant to be with each other." That, indeed, we are the messengers assigned to the task of sharing with others the message about a better way to live. As she puts it, "Our job is to mix it up. To take what we know from in here to *out there*." As long as we have people like Robyn and Tina and Dave and Harold and all of the others I have introduced you to, carrying this message, we will know a new freedom, all of us.

THE LIFE RAFT

We are promised on page 83 of the Big Book of Alcoholics Anonymous that God will begin to do for us what we have not been able to do for ourselves. What it doesn't specifically say is that God does this partly through the auspices of the sponsor we have chosen. We get the strength we need when we need it by having someone present in our life who will walk with us through our fears. Sponsors offer us the hope of their own experience when we can't manufacture any for ourselves. They remind us that "this too will pass" whenever we feel overwhelmed by the circumstances of our life. A sponsor's help is one of the ways we experience God acting in our lives.

One of the most important realizations for the newcomer is how much alike we are. Most of us come into the program certain of our uniqueness. Although we begin to realize we are not so different from the other people who share their struggles in our meetings, we glean this understanding of our sameness more emphatically through our deep conversations with our sponsors, who tell us stories of their journey to get and stay sober. This one-to-one communication is the life raft that will see us through the most troubling of times.

I have mentioned the importance of different perspectives before, but I want to highlight it. One of the key distinctions of our disease is our willfulness. This generally manifests as our having the "only right opinion" on whatever topic is under discussion. This closed-mindedness is a pretty unattractive characteristic, and through the guidance of a sponsor, we are led to see, and in time even appreciate, that another person has a view based on an individual experience that is also valid. How does the sponsor get this idea across to us? My sponsor reminded me frequently of how close to death I had come during my isolated, using days and how well informed I now was as the result of joining with and listening to other people share their experience, strength, and hope, which in each case grew out of an experience that was unique to them. Learning to trust that we each have the specific experiences we need to take this path to full recovery teaches us that our path is not the specific path for everyone, and that different perspectives growing out of different experiences are the natural result.

One of the mysteries of this disease is its randomness. No one is guaranteed immunity. The circumstances you were born into don't matter. Nor can the disease be counted on to skip a person because of "good works." On the other hand, it occasionally skips whole generations, and it can skip a single person in a family even when the others are experiencing the dramatic effects of the disease. We are all aware that particular cultural groups are devastated by the disease, and there is no absolute scientific explanation for this other than genetics. The next story is an example of this legacy.

FIFTEEN

MANY PATHS OF FREEDOM

MARY JANE'S STORY

Mary Jane was one of sixteen kids born to an alcoholic mom and dad. She remembers them as loving parents even though alcohol was always present and ruining the lives of the entire family. One of her fondest memories of her mother is watching her at the ironing board. Her mother ironed everything, and with sixteen children she was often standing there. When she wasn't ironing for her own family, she was ironing for someone else's family for the income it offered. Mary Jane repeats the pattern she learned from her mother. Every morning, she irons what she will wear that day. Mary Jane told me that ironing is a form of meditation for her; she feels better about the day she is facing if she meditates in this manner before getting into the thick of it.

Before the disease claimed the lives of both her parents (they died in their early fifties), state authorities took custody of the children. All sixteen were removed from their home on the reservation, split up into small groups, and placed in foster care. Mary Jane was allowed to stay with her younger sister and her slightly older brother in the home that was selected for them. The real horror of her life began in this setting.

Mary Jane was terrified at being torn from her parents and taken to a strange environment to live with people she had never met before. She tried to act brave so her younger sister wouldn't be so scared, but her bravery was a lie. From their first night in this home, she knew that their stay was going to be difficult, far more difficult than living with a mom and dad who were often drunk or not at home. At least with them, she experienced no physical abuse. That was not to be the case in this foster home, as became clear the very first night. Mary Jane didn't know what to do or how they would survive this experience. She was far too young to be able to sort out their options, if there were any.

It hadn't mattered to the state authorities that none of the children wanted to leave the only home they had known. It hadn't mattered that their parents had never abused them physically. The love between parents and children was evident to anyone who wanted to see it, but nothing mattered. The decision had been made. They were separated and sent to live with uncaring foster parents who were collecting money for their so-called care.

DEEP SCARS

One of the deepest hurts during these early months was that the children didn't know the whereabouts of one another. This was no doubt an intentional decision by the state. This situation was deeply painful for sixteen children who had grown accustomed to looking out for one another and who had never doubted the love of their parents. It hadn't mattered that their parents were often absent from the home. They knew they would return, always. Now, they did not know if they would ever see their parents or one another again.

Mary Jane tried her best to watch over her younger sister. Her brother seemed able to take care of himself, even though he had grown sullen and distant, which worried Mary Jane. She understands now, as a grown woman, that his sullenness was the result of feeling that he should have been able to protect Mary Jane and Sandy from the abuse they were experiencing at the hands of the foster parents, but that was impossible. He felt like a failure; he was beginning to display behavior reminiscent of their father's.

Mary Jane ran away for the first time after just a few months in that home. She didn't want to leave her little sister behind, but she couldn't take the abuse any longer. Watching what was happening to her little sister felt even worse than what was happening to herself. She felt powerless, and her shame over not being able to help her sister was overwhelming. So she ran. She didn't get far, of course. She wasn't gone long. The authorities found her, and she paid a big price for "her incorrigibility." But that didn't keep her from running again and again.

Attempting to escape was Mary Jane's pattern for a few years. More than one foster home gave her reason to run. At age sixteen, she even managed to get a few hundred miles away. She simply found no compassion, no contentment, and certainly no love in any one of the homes. Eventually, she was left to her own devices for survival. No more foster homes. No more parenting. By this time, she had begun to mimic the drinking patterns of the parents she had been torn from while still a child.

For a number of years Mary Jane had no regular contact with most of her siblings. She didn't even know where some of them were. And she had little energy to find out. She was surviving to the best of her ability on her own, sometimes on the street, other times in the home of someone she barely knew. The alcohol helped her forget her past as well as her present. The first of her five children, a girl, was born during this phase of her life. Miraculously, none of Mary Jane's children have been afflicted with fetal alcohol syndrome, though all of them were at risk.

In my talks with Mary Jane I could see how she had managed to survive. Not only was she exceptionally smart about life on the street and the dangers lurking there, but she also had a mind full of knowledge about many topics. Even though she had not had access to a college education, she was educated in myriad ways. She can problem-solve easily and she is creative. Her years on the street, drinking, hiding, and running, didn't destroy her intellect. Her gifts have enabled Mary Jane to be a loving contributor to the lives of those around her today.

LOST TO THE DISEASE

The grace that has saved Mary Jane thus far skipped over many of her siblings, however. This continues to cause her excruciating pain. Why me? she wonders, aloud and in the silence of her mind. The family's pain is the reason she resumed drinking on far too many occasions. As I listened to her story, I marveled that she had managed to return to the program so many times. I also realized there was no guarantee that her trips were over. She certainly didn't want to repeat her pattern any longer, but the pull to chemicals was sometimes exceedingly great, especially if the life of another sibling or niece or nephew was lost to the disease, as had just happened shortly before we last talked.

Suicide was a common theme in Mary Jane's family of origin, beginning with her father, who finally put a gun to his head and pulled the trigger at the age of fifty-two because he simply could not stop drinking. The most recent death among her siblings was to suicide, too. The younger sister she tried to care for in their first of many foster homes ended her life with the help of alcohol and too many pills. It was suicide. She left a note. There was no way Mary Jane could have prevented it, but she mourns and carries the ache of their past together into every experience of her life today.

How do you keep moving forward when so many tragedies have befallen your family? Having five children and two grandchildren helps. So does having a score of nieces and nephews whom you want to save from having to trudge the path of addiction. Mary Jane spends many hours trying to steer family members away from the allure of drugs and alcohol. No one knows better than she that the allure is a dead-end street.

There are many incidents about her life that Mary Jane shared with me that are too horrific to share with you here, particularly the stories about the sexual, physical, and emotional abuse she experienced at the hands of those being paid to care for her. Suffice it to say that at least up until the time of our interview, she was destined to be a survivor. She doesn't doubt that the hand of God saved her life. What sometimes troubles her, though, is why she and her siblings had to experience any of the trauma they experienced. Where was the hand of God then?

Despite that troubling question, Mary Jane's faith is bolstered by a particular memory: the time she was discovered and saved when she was so drunk she didn't know her own name, where she was, where she lived, or who to call. The last thing she remembered that chilly spring day was being in a bar. She knows she went there in the late afternoon, as was her custom during that period of relapse, and that's all she remembers. The couple who came to her rescue had rescued her many times before, but this time was different.

A LATE-NIGHT CRY FOR HELP

Mary Jane recounted for me the story the couple told her about that night. It is surely evidence of "the hand of God." Their phone rang in the late evening and there was nothing but garbled words on the other end of the line. Kay heard them and suspected it was Mary Jane, but not until another voice came on the line was she sure it was Mary Jane. The voice said, "If you know this drunken Indian, come and get her. She is so drunk she can't walk or talk. We'll get her outside of our restaurant some way but if you don't get here soon, we are calling the police."

Kay drove to the restaurant to get Mary Jane and struggled to get her into her van, no easy feat because Mary Jane was overweight and nearly immobile in her drunken state. She didn't recognize Kay. She couldn't speak. She was angry and physically violent. Kay got her husband and a neighbor to help get Mary Jane out of the car and into the house. There she raged all night, wailing the words of Indian songs in her native tongue, beating her legs as though they were drums, a mournful sound that filled Kay and Dan's house.

Mary Jane went to treatment for the fifth time after this experience. She didn't want to go. She had tried this method of stopping drinking more than once and had had only limited success, but something about the experience of dialing Kay's phone when she wasn't able to speak her own name, or even recognize Kay when she arrived, gave her the sense that the hand of someone else was present in her life. She knew in a deep inner place in her being that she had been saved and she came to believe, with the help of Kay and then her counselor in treatment, that she had been saved for a reason she might never understand.

But her drinking had come to an end. She stayed sober for nearly eighteen months after this particular treatment; however, for nearly half of those months she lived in a halfway house, which made the commitment to sobriety easier. But she wandered back to the familiar bars not long after returning home.

Amazingly, Mary Jane never lost a job, nor did she lose her home, her kids, or her husband throughout this series of treatments, relapses, and disappearances. Just as she had run from many foster homes when she was a kid, she periodically ran away from home as an adult, not because she was the target of sexual or physical abuse, but because she was an alcoholic who repeatedly lost her way.

Mary Jane's husband was in recovery, which made it both harder and easier for her. Because he was sober, the two kids still at home were never neglected, even when she was gone for long periods of time, whether in treatment, in a halfway house, or on the run, but his own sobriety had come so much easier to him that it made it impossible for him to accept or understand why hers was constantly eluding her. The anger he had was palpable; the kids could see it and feel it. But they loved Mary Jane and didn't know where to place their loyalty when the tension was present between their parents.

The saddest result of Mary Jane's circumstances is that her youngest children, ages twelve and fifteen, continue to suffer confusion over who is the "good parent" and who is the bad. Whether the disease will personally claim their lives isn't apparent yet, but their lives have certainly been adversely affected. Mary Jane is sad that this is the case, but the past cannot be erased. Nor can she be certain she won't repeat much of it again. She can only say that for today she is clean and sober. Not one of us reading this can promise more than this.

GRACED WITH SOBRIETY

What a terrible disease we suffer from. But the recovery, while we are in it, is as profound as the disease is terrible. Mary Jane is in recovery at the current time. Her story reminds us that grace is offered to us with no strings attached. Mary Jane was graced with many periods of sobriety or she wouldn't be alive right now.

As I reflect on the many sadnesses of her life, juxtaposed with the many lives she has influenced in a positive way, I sense that her journey, including all of her relapses, has been part of the divine picture chosen for her. We are always in the right place at the right time. Even when that place is full of pain, we can take something good away from it that will inform our own journey in the future, or the journey of someone who will come to us for guidance.

The disease, in some form, attacked all fifteen of Mary Jane's siblings. In her own case, she surrendered control to more than alcohol. She gave her life over to crack cocaine on occasion, too. When she talked about this part of her addiction, I could tell that she was astounded at how quickly crack claimed her mind. She said it took only a couple of rocks to stimulate her craving again and again. She said there was nothing like it. When she was caught in the cycle, she could think of nothing else but getting some more.

I am amazed she got free of its clutches. I sense that she is, too. It occurs to me that her alcohol relapses don't seem to be as big a deal to her now because they are familiar, not as all-consuming, and more easily "controlled." She has relapsed many times and she has sobered up even more times, as have many of her siblings. I think she is terrified that if she used crack cocaine again, even once, she might never come back. This is a healthy fear.

I mentioned earlier that Mary Jane's family has been devastated by this disease. It's important to also note that at the present time, she has three sober sisters and three sober brothers, although one of the brothers is sober only because he is no longer capable of living alone or caring for his own needs. The other brothers and sisters are now at rest, in the care of the Great Spirit. Nine members of Mary Jane's immediate family are dead and alcohol was the killer. How many of us have experienced such loss?

And the disease isn't finished with the family. The next generation is a repeat performance of the previous two. There have been suicides, prison terms, many treatments, and many more relapses among the nieces and nephews. The saddest part of Mary Jane's life now is watching the disease chase after the next generation. It waits in the shadows to attack, and it never misses the target. Mary Jane keeps showing up to pick up the remains and the circle goes on.

Mary Jane is clean and sober today, or was when this was written. She knows, and I came to know, too, that her sobriety may always be a tentative thing. There are no guarantees with Mary Jane when it comes to this disease. The same can be said for the rest of us. However, those of us who cling to Alcoholics Anonymous have a better chance of dying sober.

Mary Jane has not been able to grab the program except for brief periods of time. Nor have her sober siblings taken this particular path to sobriety. Because Alcoholics Anonymous worked for me, I struggled not to be "preachy" with Mary Jane when we talked. She assured me she heard the speech from a number of her friends and former sponsors quite often. She had tried AA. At times she had liked AA. But in the final analysis it didn't speak to her as it speaks to many of us.

Celebrating her sobriety on whatever path works for her is the real message of Mary Jane's story. She has been graced to experience sobriety just as you and I have been graced. And she has helped others find it, if only for brief stints. Who can say that one path to freedom is better than another? The fact that many of us are being used or have been used to lead another person down a sober path is all that matters. The angels in disguise are everywhere, on every path, looking for any sign of trouble in our lives. I am convinced, even more so after collecting all of the stories for this book, that they got us here. And they will help us stay here if that's our choice.

Mary Jane's story and her current sobriety had a deep impact on me. I was moved to tears many times as she spoke to me. I kept wanting to ask, "Why?" And I knew every time I silently asked it, there was no answer. God doesn't do this to us. But God is always available to lead us out, sometimes through the extended hand of a stranger, sometimes through a message we read in a book, and most frequently through the quiet knowing in our own minds when we ask for help.

In Mary Jane's case, it was probably the combination of all three, but Kay and her husband were certainly instrumental. Mary Jane needed and deserved the extra care they offered. She had had so little parenting throughout her life. They offered the kind of attention, love, and care she craved. The sad part is always that no matter how hard the "parent" tries, he or she can't give "the child" what they want her to have. They can only pray and hope and hold the image of a loving outcome for the child in their minds. The actual outcome isn't theirs to guarantee.

This book is a collection of stories revealing the crucial role of sponsors on the paths of recovering people. But as is apparent, especially in Mary Jane's story, not all sponsors are "friends of Bill W." All sponsors are doing the work of God, however, and lives are saved, journeys are influenced, histories are changed, and every person alive is affected in the total scheme of life. Profound is the impact that the actions of one can have.

THE ROLE OF FAITH

So much has to be accepted on faith. It is certainly no accident that Bill W. and Dr. Bob concluded that developing a belief in God, *as we understand Him,* was necessary if we were to get firmly on this path and remain here. Their own lives had informed them every step of the way. Neither was able to take in the information early enough to prevent the many brushes with death they both experienced as a result of their drinking, but then the time was finally right and their paths crossed. We, you and I, sharing this message, are the outcome! Whenever I quiet my mind and remember again the evolution of this fellowship, I am stunned. There is no doubt in my mind at that moment that every outcome to every challenge is already known to God. We simply have to walk our way toward it, trusting that we will be told the solution to any situation that troubles us when it is our time to know it. Faith will soften any blow.

Sponsors can intercede in many ways in our lives. We have seen evidence of this in every story shared here. What also is apparent, at least to me, and even more so since gathering these stories, is that there are no chance encounters, ever. Every encounter, when examined with an open heart, can be seen as God's gift offered to us as part of our education. What we generally resist is the notion that not all experiences (which will in time be interpreted for our good) need to feel good when we are in the flow of their unfolding. But healing is taking place within each experience if we fully embrace the experience. Let me repeat again, *faith will soften any blow.*

There are so many gifts we receive from sponsorship, regardless of which end of sponsorship we are on. As mentioned before, being the one meting out the suggestions, the sponsor receives the most immediate help from the exchange of ideas. My own experiences with sponsees have taught me repeatedly that what I share with another woman is always what I need to remember, *one more time,* for my own journey. The listener may or may not be ready to hear the solution to a problem when it is offered.

How fortunate that *the solution waits for us until we are ready to experience it.* This can reduce one's fear of not understanding God's will in a particular situation. Just because we can't decipher it instantly doesn't mean we will have missed our single opportunity. It will be held for us until we are ready to embrace it. Our lives do make sense! They have at their very core a spiritual purpose. Even when we don't feel spiritual or even embrace the idea of spirituality, we are on a specific, divine journey. Now we can see this clearly. Isn't it awesome?

I have given a great deal of thought to the many miracles I became privy to while listening to the stories I have shared with you here. My understanding and acceptance of the idea that God is always "in the wings" to do for us what we can't do for ourselves has been strengthened tenfold. I am hopeful that the same has been true for you in reading these stories. I feel my encounters with the storytellers were *holy* encounters, that I was on a mission from God even though I didn't know this when the process began.

WHEN OUR HELP IS REJECTED

There is another aspect of the sponsorship relationship that needs to be addressed: How should the sponsor respond when she or he tries to offer help or guidance and it is flatly refused, argued with, or ignored? Particularly when the sponsee has sought guidance, it isn't easy to accept the sponsee's refusal of the help. But that's the only response one can make. We are not in the relationship as the "controller" of it, although many of us would prefer this role. Our part in the relationship is simply to offer suggestions that will be accepted or rejected. We do not get to determine what happens next.

My personal bias is that the program of Al-Anon has a lot to teach all of us about control. Its premise is how to let go of the others in our lives. And others are everywhere. I have heard it said many times, and my own sponsor told me this when I first got sober, that most relapses occur because of relationships going sour.

The most obvious reason for relationships going sour is that control of another person doesn't work. The best way I have found to learn about letting go of control of someone else's life is through the fellowship of Al-Anon. We need to learn, not only on behalf of our sponsees, but on behalf of everyone sharing our journey, that it isn't our prerogative to control them. This doesn't mean we won't want to. It doesn't mean we won't try. It simply means it is not our job to control others. In time, we will even be grateful that it isn't. "We will know a new freedom," as the promises so aptly reveal.

Sponsorship teaches us much more than just learning how to let go. It also teaches us some skills we hadn't even imagined it would. For instance, I learned some important things about time management from being a sponsor. This may sound strange, but the reality is that all of us are busy with the important as well as the mundane activities that call to us daily. Adding to this mix of responsibilities the commitment we have made to being a sponsor to one person, or perhaps many people, means we have to set priorities for what gets our attention on a daily basis.

Early in my own recovery I loved being asked to be a sponsor. I still love sponsorship, in fact, but for different reasons now. Particularly in the early days, sponsorship gave my own recovery a greater purpose. I needed to feel that my past counted for *something* good since I still had so much shame around it. But my readiness to be a sponsor to too many people quickly distracted me from my own recovery needs. The outcome was that I got off track, and was not a great help to anyone. My own sponsor then suggested that I needed to manage my time better, to determine what I needed to do for myself each day, and then, and only then, commit to spending time in person or on the phone with a sponsee. This began a pattern of behavior for me that is still helpful and extremely effective. I don't feel good about anything if I don't accomplish some of the tasks on my own to-do list on a daily basis. If I give all of my time to others, I begin to resent the sponsees, and all of us are harmed by my attitude. Doing for others what I can, after doing for myself what I must, offers the best accommodation to all of us.

I have mentioned before the value of exploring differing perspectives when confronted by a dilemma of any kind in our sobriety. This is particularly the case when we talk about the spiritual dimension of this program. Many of us came into the fellowship turned off by formal religion. Many either doubted the existence of God or considered him to be a punishing God, regardless of the religious training we might have had in the past. The troubles that seemed to follow us wherever we went before we ended up in recovery made our skepticism seem pretty rational.

Hearing from others in the meetings that we can interpret God however it suits us frees us to take our time with the "God Steps." Good sponsors will reiterate that our recovery is a process; our understanding of the principles of this program is a process, too. Developing a relationship with a Higher Power, however we experience that Power, is the most important process of all. Listening to a sponsor tell how he or she "came to believe" will open our minds and hearts to the most rewarding aspect of this new way of life.

Enough can never be said about the importance of our spiritual growth. Fortunately we don't have to do this part overnight. Being surrounded by men and women who share in the necessary belief that cultivating a spiritual connection to God and to one another in this program, as well as in the community at large, is all the impetus most of us need to do likewise. Sponsorship shows us how to do this.

SIXTEEN

HONORING A NEW WAY OF LIFE

THOMAS'S STORY

The journey to freedom is a long one for most addicts. This was certainly true for Thomas. His journey began at age eleven. Beer and Pepsi mixed was his first drug of choice. He said he hated the taste of beer but he liked the effects. Mixing it with Pepsi made it possible to get it down. The first time he drank he felt sure that it made him more acceptable to his peers. That's really all it took for him to continue the journey.

Thomas was the second of five boys born to parents ill-equipped to raise children well. They had married at age sixteen, hardly more than children themselves. Thomas's father thought that all problems could best be handled with his fists, and he used them often on everyone in the family. It wasn't a pleasant home life, nor did it offer much hope for a pleasant future. Thomas followed his peers into lawbreaking activities, not an unusual response, considering the patterns in his home. Car theft under the influence of alcohol was common with Thomas and his friends. He remembers feeling scared and guilty, but not enough to quit the behavior. He also remembers how glad he was that his dad didn't catch him. The beating would have been unmerciful.

It was in high school that Thomas branched out into marijuana and glue sniffing. They were great accompaniments for his drinking, which had not subsided. He and his brother played in a rock band, and both boys, often drunk and drugged, fit the image of rock stars in the sixties and seventies. The Vietnam War was raging and the band was screaming against it. Being high was a chosen way of life for Thomas. His fears about dying in a foreign country, fighting a war he didn't understand, fueled his resolve to stay high. So did the fact that his dad was in the National Guard and hated hippies, hated war protesters, and hated rock music.

When he was a senior in high school, the family moved to Florida. The biggest thrill about this move was that alcohol was legal there for eighteen-year-olds at that time. Thomas and his brother couldn't wait to legally buy that first bottle of Seagrams. Thomas wanted to be in charge of something. Now he could at least be in charge of when, how often, and how much he drank. He had wanted to be in charge of lots of other things in the past with no success. One of the stories he shared with me poignantly reveals this. He desperately wanted a girlfriend and finally found one. He sees now that he took her hostage from the very first date. To keep her his hostage, he even resorted to self-mutilation. He cut the palms of his hands to get her attention, in the hopes that it would bind her to him. The dysfunction in both of their lives greatly complicated their journeys.

Thomas was an Elvis fan and was deluded enough to think that if he was good enough on the guitar, girls would want him just as they wanted Elvis. He was mistaken, but the alcohol and drugs fueled his delusion for many years. Living in Florida was a plus; it made the fuel legal. His first real job was cleaning bathrooms. He quickly moved up to supervisor, after his own boss was fired for drinking scotch on the job. Thomas continued the practice he'd learned from his boss of secretly drinking on the job.

With money in his pockets, Thomas made connections in the drug world easily. He had recreated the world he had left behind when he moved to Florida, and he relished it. Soon he married his "hostage," and they honeymooned in Key West, an experience he will long remember. A wedding night when he was too drunk to even acknowledge his wife was followed by a gigantic hangover that he barely survived while riding around Key West on the Conch Train. Thomas was so sick that he couldn't drink for two days. How glad he was that he had pot to keep him high when he was too sick to drink.

Drugs and alcohol were Thomas's constant companions. They kept him functional for his heavy schedule of working full time and attending college. To all of this he added a commitment to dieting and working out. He had been overweight his whole life and was intent on getting thin. With the help of a prescription drug and the workouts, he lost a hundred pounds.

REPEAT PERFORMANCE

At about this time, his wife got pregnant. When their first child was born, Thomas stayed clean and sober for a few days, the first sober, clean period he had had since his drugging journey began. It was a great way to honor the birth of his first child, but it didn't last. Being high was his preferred way of life. Whether on his job or in school, being high was no problem. He was the supervisor on the job, and being high in classes was not unusual in the college setting. Thomas fit right in.

The next few years were a repeat performance. A second

child was born, the last for them, which meant Thomas was finally free from worry over possible birth defects as the result of his drug use. Of course, worrying had not kept him from using whatever drug was handy, but now he felt exonerated. PCP, cocaine, and heroin were added to his list of choices, all in an attempt to recapture the feeling he had had the first time he was high, but nothing dulled the inner pain. His search for the perfect high continued, however.

Martial arts contributed to Thomas's physical fitness. His self-image had improved to the extent that he now felt ready to pursue other women. His life was spinning out of control, but he couldn't see it. His employer could, however, and after wrecking one of their vans while drunk, Thomas was fired. His drug use was now so heavy that he needed more than one job to support it. Unfortunately, he couldn't clothe and feed his kids and keep himself high. Getting high was his priority. Life was dismal for Thomas's family. Being high didn't allow Thomas to successfully escape the pain, either. He attempted suicide twice to escape it, but failed. The pain won.

A couple more lost jobs led to the decision to move back to Ohio and his home town. The geographic cure didn't work. In fact, it only led to a search for stronger drugs, this time legal, over-the-counter drugs. The one he abused first was for migraine headaches. He eventually took twelve to twenty of them every day. They made him mean and unstable. He was scared enough by their effects to quit them, but before he did, he got two bottles of one hundred from his supplier and took sixty of them in a five-hour period one day. That night, he went into convulsions, wet the bed, and had an out-of-body experience, or so it seemed to him. He felt surrounded by Spirit and was offered some choices to change his life. He wanted to make them.

A MOMENT OF SANITY

Upon awakening, he felt like a stranger in his body. He cried out to his wife for help. In a moment of sanity, he knew he needed help, more help than she alone could give. While still lying in bed, his four-year-old daughter came into the bedroom and began picking up his pills from under the bed. They were his aspirins, he told her, just as he had told her on many previous occasions, as he began popping them into his mouth, trying to stabilize himself enough to make it to the hospital. Thomas's twenty-eight-day treatment for alcoholism began at this point.

He wasn't in treatment with any serious goals for the future. He didn't really know why he was there, even though he knew he needed help, and he had no expectations of what he might get out of the experience. What happened on the fourth day, therefore, took him very much by surprise. He began to feel a Power much larger than himself come into his life. There were no bright lights and no music, just the quiet knowing that from this day forward something would be different. Most of us long for a dramatic spiritual awakening, but few of us have one. The *knowing* that Thomas experienced is far more familiar.

From that day forward, life has appeared different to Thomas, and his way of interacting in the world is very different. He still wonders why the Presence came to him, but he no longer doubts that he deserves it. He knows that he has been asked to share with others what has been given to him. The Twelve Steps and Twelve Traditions have profoundly influenced his life. Honesty was unknown to Thomas. He never saw the value in it. One might say, he never saw the value in doing anything that was for the betterment of the world and the people around him. His entire existence, from the time he drank that first beer mixed with Pepsi, had been to recreate and then maintain the high he had felt the first time. It was never to happen. As was the case for most of us, the rapture eluded him, again and again, but the chase continued.

Thomas doesn't recall a particular individual coming into his life with the message that was to change his life forever. Certainly his wife getting him to the hospital, with help from her dad, was crucial. And the doctor who convinced him that what he needed was treatment for drug and alcohol use counts, too. But a startling experience wasn't the catalyst. His "rebirth" was not like the one I experienced with Pat when she knocked on my door and averted me from suicide. That's the fascinating thing about our journeys, not just Thomas's and mine, but all of our journeys. We each came to experience a new perspective, a new plan for living in a specific way, a way that was divinely right for us.

BABY STEPS

Everything about Thomas's life appeared different now. He felt as though he saw with new eyes. Never before had he seen colors so bright, trees so plentifully clothed with leaves, and ripe, wild fruit beneath his feet all around him in the fields close by. He wondered if all of this was there before, or had the countryside been "reborn" along with him? As has happened to so many of us when we first got clean and sober, Thomas was in awe of what he saw. Every day he saw new and beautiful sights, but none more beautiful than his four-year-old daughter and six-year-old son. They loved him unconditionally; they had always loved him unconditionally, even when he was stoned and unavailable, and they taught him what that meant. They were his most loving teachers.

With his wife, a lot of repair work was needed. The unconditional love was less forthcoming. She had borne the brunt of his brutality for the many years of their marriage. She didn't plan to leave, but she wasn't eager to stay without some significant changes in their relationship. Thomas was willing to make them. Baby steps came first. In time, the mending was evident. He wanted to be a responsible mate. He has learned that responsibility is unending. Our work on this is never over. Most of us reach a point in recovery when we are glad to realize we always have an assignment like this. It means we have a reason for getting up each morning.

But not all growth is fun. Growth can be painful. We are told early on by members of the fellowship that pain and gain go hand in hand. While this is not an absolute truth, it does happen this way much of the time. What members of the fellowship also assure us is that no pain has to be tolerated alone. Others in the fellowship are always willing to listen when our need is to talk, and God is always as close as our nearest next thought. Our path is one of growth, and it will come to us in myriad ways. Our path throughout our lives has been one of growth; not until getting clean and sober have we been able to celebrate it fully. The growth we might have been making before our recovery was often shadowed by the traumas that resulted from our drinking.

What a different life we now live. It's not likely that anyone reading this book could have imagined this journey a few short years ago. Certainly that is true for me. Now I can imagine no other. Thomas shares this feeling. Why does it take us so long to get here? But if we got here more easily and with fewer traumas, would we appreciate what the program gives us? Perhaps not.

A SPIRITUAL PROGRAM

Like many of us, Thomas is convinced that what has changed in his life the most is the spiritual part of this program. His belief system is entirely new as the result of the journey. What made the biggest difference to him is that no one dictated what his spiritual journey needed to be. He had the freedom to create what fit for him. And it keeps changing just as he keeps changing.

Thomas relied on no single sponsor to show him the way when he came into our fellowship. It is suggested by most of us and by the program literature that it is best if we do rely on a specific sponsor, especially when we first get clean and sober. But we all have the freedom to do the program however it fits for us, and Thomas relied on the meetings, the socializing before and after the meetings, the general discussion that happened at every meeting, and the literature about our disease and the recovery from it. The combination of all of these elements showed him how to change his life. As he so aptly put it, "Life was never this exciting before recovery." The possibilities for change, new experiences, and new opportunities to live this message are everywhere.

Carrying the program with us into every experience is the most important thing we can do. The principles we have learned to live by are worthy of emulation by everyone we come into contact with on a daily basis. It's not by accident that the Twelfth Step suggests that we do exactly this. Many of us have come to believe that members of this fellowship are indeed the way-showers for the rest of humanity. If we can demonstrate to others that there is value in kindness, honesty, willingness to listen, and commitment to a spiritual journey, we will have nurtured a new perspective that can be seen and appreciated by others. Thomas demonstrates this ably. His every thought is steeped in Twelve Step living, he says, and this makes every moment of his life a joy to experience.

One of the circumstances that had to occur in Thomas's life in order for him to truly commit to this "simple program" was to divorce his family of origin. He didn't make this decision lightly. He tried for a number of years to stay in contact, but the games continued. They refused to honor his new life, and the unpleasant experiences with them that ensued hung on in his mind for weeks after they were over. The toll they were taking was not just hard on him but on his family, too, and he decided to make the break.

In the process, he and his wife decided to change their name. After years of cringing over his surname because of the bank of awful childhood and adult memories, Thomas and his wife changed their last name to one they feel fits them. Now when their name is called, they raise their heads proudly and feel ready to go forth to do the work of the Great Spirit that has done so much work on their behalf.

Thomas ended his story by saying that the Mystery walking with him is with each of us. He relishes the fact that life is a continuum and that the end will never come. He relishes also the fact that each new day is the only one that matters, and that he will not be walking through it alone. He has conveyed this knowledge to his children as well. Together, Thomas and his family are wonderful examples of a fully recovering family. Just a few years ago, they were destined for a life of poverty, at best, or total abandonment to the streets at worst. But because of a series of circumstances, beginning with a "dream" that Thomas had during his final, most debilitating drunk, he and his family have rediscovered each other and have discovered what a good life is available to them now. We get here through a multitude of ways. Thomas's way was not like anyone else's. But he arrived safely, nonetheless. That's the miracle.

AN OFTEN OFFERED MESSAGE

Have you ever stopped to consider the role your various sponsors have played? Do you, occasionally, say a silent prayer on their behalf? Without them none of us would be here. Our willingness to finally listen to the suggestions of others is what made our journey possible. Do you ever wonder why you were willing to listen that time in particular? For the majority of us, similar words had been spoken to us on many occasions, but we were unable to let them penetrate. Then they did, and we stopped moving along the path that had become our habitual one. We chose again. And here we are.

I am certain there are those who would say our quitting is coincidental or an act of willpower or something that simply happened. But we know otherwise. We are here because of a divine intervention by a particular person who was listening to his or her inner voice and sharing those words, those prayers, with us. It was our time for a new direction and we were ready. We were finally ready.

When two are gathered together, God makes it three. That's the safety net that is available to all of us if we reach for it. Instead of sitting in our pain, in isolation, we can seek solace from another person, and God will join us. This axiom is true for every member of the human race. We have not been singled out to receive a gift that's unavailable to others. But the gift that is being offered to us, the gift of sobriety, is special to our specific needs. To many it is offered, but few accept.

Do you ever wonder why this is so? I have known scores of people who have declined the offer. I am sure you have known many, too. Can they not see the changes that have occurred in our lives? At times I am haunted by the question, Why me and not them? But it isn't up to us to answer this question. It has become our job to represent the sober life, to silently advertise it, so to speak. This is a program of attraction, not promotion, and we are the symbols of what life can be for others who need sobriety. Our role is significant. Even if we never specifically sponsored any one, even if we never did a Twelfth Step with a suffering addict, we will still have done our job well by staying clean and sober.

There are many ways to sponsor a person. When you look back on your own recovery, you will likely see the various approaches different individuals took when they interacted with you. Some were gruff and demanding. Others were quietly available and never required anything specific from you. I had one sponsor who never told me what to do, but she shared, constantly, her own journey. I learned a great deal from her by simply listening to how she handled her own struggles. I am not sure if she really knew what my specific struggles were. I know I could have shared them, and I am equally certain she would have listened. But I have never doubted that God put her in my path because of my preference for learning through listening to others, rather than asking for specifics for myself. My shame at not knowing the solutions without help was too much, so God provided the information I needed in a way that was more accessible, more palatable to me. Isn't it interesting how we always get exactly what we need?

SEVENTEEN

GOD WILL NOT GO AWAY

CINDY'S STORY

As long as we remember that we can seek help from one another to carry both the burden and the message of recovery from addiction, we will be heard by those men and women who are ready to listen. Thank goodness there were many people in Cindy's life who were willing to carry the message to her, not once but many, many times. Cindy was definitely not ready to be "called" when the message was first delivered. Cindy's background makes her particular journey understandable. Cindy was born into a family whose profession was making beer. Her father and her grandfather were German brewers. Shortly after her father came to America, he went to work in the largest brewery in this country and eventually became the senior executive. Not surprisingly, Cindy was introduced to beer while she was still a toddler.

By the age of seven, Cindy had her own glass of beer at the dinner table. In a beer-brewing family, this was not considered unusual. We might not consider it unusual, either, that Cindy's father was alcoholic. He had come from a long line of alcoholics. Though he was never treated for his alcoholism (it would have jeopardized his career), the disease didn't prevent him from succeeding in his work. Cindy's eventual alcoholism wasn't as easily handled or ignored.

When Cindy was thirteen, she traveled to Germany to visit relatives and to attend the many summer festivals. Not surprisingly, she handled her liquor as well as the old-timers, and she felt proud when they praised her. She was following in the footsteps of her ancestors and liked her experiences. By age fifteen she was mixing drinks for her mom and downing a few herself. Socializing meant going to a lot of parties in high school, and she selected those she would attend by the kind and prevalence of liquor that would likely be present. She didn't waste her time going where no booze would be available.

Cindy is certain she had crossed the line to being a full-blown alcoholic by the time she was seventeen. She went to college in California, far enough away from home that she could hide her frequent drinking more easily. As a matter of course, she had two cases of beer delivered to her dorm every week. She came to school with fake identification. Drinking had become a part of her life at such an early age that it didn't even register on her mind that her dorm friends didn't join in the drinking as eagerly as Cindy.

In her third year of college, Cindy went abroad to study. Her focus was so much on alcohol that she made few friends. Before long she was suffering from both loneliness and depression. Vodka had become her drug of choice, and her primary relationship was with the bottle, which sat prominently on her nightstand. Cindy turned to it whenever she felt in need of comfort, which was often. She recognized now that she was like her dad, and she accepted this as her state in life.

When she returned to this country, she went to a psychiatrist, seeking help for her troubled mind. Never did he probe into her drinking habits. Cindy offered no information, either, and nothing changed, except that she had become addicted to marijuana, too. In spite of her alcoholism, drug addiction, and depression, she was resilient and graduated from college. She returned to her home town after graduation but didn't stay long. She sought the glamour of a big city and moved to New York, where she took a secretarial course so that she could get a job. Her liberal arts education hadn't prepared her for the only work available there. Cindy developed a taste for martinis and felt like a sophisticated New Yorker in no time.

A GLIMPSE OF SOBRIETY

After a couple of years in New York, Cindy had an opportunity to join a ship's crew of seventeen and sail to the Galapagos Islands. She had never crewed before but was game for any adventure. She was at sea for three months, which proved to be quite an adventure for an addict who was accustomed to drinking alcohol and smoking pot every day. The brief stints in port were welcome reliefs to her. What she did discover was that her depression lifted while out at sea. Cindy didn't connect this with the absence of alcohol, but she certainly welcomed it. She also discovered that she felt more connected to people than she ever had before. Again, at the time, she didn't credit the absence of alcohol as the reason for the budding relationships. She thought it was merely because members of the crew had no one else to relate to.

Her interest in marine biology was piqued on this sail, and when the trip was over, she moved back to California to study marine biology. Her interest in it, though real, couldn't compete with her renewed interest in alcohol. Her time away from daily drinking had certainly not decreased her obsession with it, and she was soon getting so drunk, so often, that her only contacts with others were based on alcohol. Cindy met her first husband during one of these phases of drunkenness. She was trying to bike her way home from a bar they both frequented, but couldn't keep the bike upright. He saw her safely home and their romance began. Of course, he already had a wife, but that mattered not to them. He eventually followed Cindy to Los Angeles.

After his divorce, and against her parents' wishes, Cindy and Ben married and decided to build boats for a living. That neither had done anything like this before made little difference to them. Lack of experience never stops an alcoholic from dreaming the most grandiose of dreams. Surprisingly, one might even say miraculously, they did get one boat built in spite of their daily drunks. Along with the drinking, Cindy also developed a food addiction, and her weight ballooned to more than two hundred pounds. Their lives were out of control.

A GEOGRAPHIC CURE

Ironically, when they were trailering the boat to its new owner, they had a wreck and the boat was a total loss. A year's work was gone, and they were nearly penniless. They moved into a dilapidated, sixteen-foot trailer and each found work. On a trip to the desert to visit friends shortly thereafter, they were encouraged to try a new life there. Geographic cures are destined to fail, but an alcoholic never knows that when the move is undertaken. For a while, it looked like they had made the right move.

They bought a little house. Ben joined the Chamber of Commerce and learned to fly, while Cindy learned to operate a backhoe. Together they were drinking a couple of quarts of booze a day, plus beer. Ben eventually crashed his plane.

Whether he was drunk was never determined, but he did end up with brain stem damage that was permanent.

He was in the hospital for months. Upon his release, it was apparent that Cindy was often in danger in his presence. His behavior was often violent and always unpredictable. Cindy's friends were worried on her behalf, first because of Ben but also because of her drinking, which had escalated even more. For the first time, her friends suggested she go to treatment, and she did. When she was released and sober, she feared even more Ben's wrath and escaped by telling him she had to visit her sick father.

This distance between them was short-lived. So was her sobriety. Again she went to treatment. This became Cindy's pattern. She would leave Ben. He would bring her back. She would go to treatment and afterward almost immediately use again. During one relapse Cindy nearly drowned while drunk. That she survived the experience, and other near-death experiences, with no brain damage is miraculous.

Cindy continued passing through the revolving doors of detox and treatment centers for a few more years. In this span of time, she finally managed to divorce her husband, but not easily. He was enraged by her leaving and fought the divorce. She went to Alcoholics Anonymous for a time and actually got a sponsor, but still couldn't manage to stay sober. When Cindy's dad died, she had the excuse she needed to drink again. She was with him when he died. He couldn't understand her alcoholism or his own. He kept saying, "Why can't you stop drinking," never realizing that he couldn't stop, either. After his death, she went back to school in the Midwest, closer to home, but course work couldn't keep her sober. Her pattern of drinking was too ingrained. She would enter detox, go back to school, and then drink again.

When she returned to California, her mom said the most

important words she had ever spoken to Cindy: "Don't come back until you have been sober for a while." But Cindy couldn't stop drinking. She was hallucinating by now. She finally committed herself to a mental hospital out of fear, and they diagnosed her as being alcoholic and schizophrenic. She went on megavitamin drip therapy while in the hospital and then promptly drank just as soon as she was released. She tried Antabuse as a way to stop drinking but failed with that, too. No matter what she tried, Cindy drank.

Cindy next tried living in a halfway house, only to be met by failure once again. Back to treatment she went, after which she took up residence with a man she had been in the mental hospital with. They were two wounded souls. Larry's parents watched over them both, as did some of her former friends, who had lived close by while she and Ben were residing in the trailer park. Cindy didn't lack for "angels" to watch over her. She clearly sees now that many people managed to keep her alive when she didn't care if she stayed alive or not.

STILL NOT READY

Treatment did little more than keep Cindy sober for the few weeks she was there. When I listened to her story, I was shocked at how completely she failed to hear the message that was being offered to her. She was not ready. Period. We do not hear the message until it's truly our time to hear it. Had I ever really doubted this, my doubts would have been dispelled by Cindy's story. She went into treatment yet again and then into another halfway house, and upon release returned to what she knew best. Before long she was living in fleabag motels when she wasn't on the street.

Again she went north to try treatment one more time. This program was tough, considered tougher than most, and her friends' hopes were high. Much to the utter dismay of them all, Cindy went right back to the streets, some nights sleeping at the YWCA, some nights simply hanging around the bars close to the Greyhound station, secretly hoping someone would kill her since she didn't have the courage to jump off the bridge. The only message that kept ringing in Cindy's ears was one she heard in one of her many treatments: "If a million alcoholics can't recover, what makes you think you can?" In fact, she didn't think she could. Not ever.

But the tables were about to turn for Cindy. Her last drink was with the director of the YWCA, after which she called a woman she had once met, whose number she carried with her, to ask for help. Why she was willing to make the call continues to baffle her. How she even remembered she had the number still baffles her, too. She had never been willing to call before. She doesn't recall if anything actually felt different. She simply made the call and the woman who answered gave her the number of another woman, a recovering counselor, who could help.

Cindy called Jane. That call, in turn, led Cindy to detox yet one more time, followed by treatment and ultimately a long-term care facility where she heard *the message* at last. As Cindy was retelling this part of her story, I could easily sense how certain she was that God had been trying to intervene at many points along her path. But she was ready when she was ready, and not a moment before.

She was employed by the long-term care facility when she "graduated" from it, and she sustained the only sobriety she had ever really had. She continues to sustain it, and so many others have benefited by her abstinence these past eighteen years because she has given her life, through her profession now, to the sobriety of others. Cindy went to the seminary to become a chaplain a dozen years ago and now has her own facility for people who are seeking a spiritual solution for the struggles they face on life's pathway.

THE LIFE FORCE

That she could be doing what she is currently doing profoundly amazes Cindy, me, and her many friends and family members along the way who tried to help her. There is no doubt in her mind that Cindy was reborn. The life force was so great that none of her attempts to destroy it could succeed. That's how she knows that when others come to her for help, it's the inner voice that has spoken to them, a voice that she recognizes from her own past.

She well remembers her intake interview when she entered her last treatment facility. Lily, the counselor, asked her about her significant relationships. Cindy responded that her significant other was God. Where those words came from, she still isn't sure. She had no conscious understanding of what they meant at the time. But they provided the turning point for her life. She and Lily both knew from that moment on that Cindy's sober trip was about to begin.

When we talked and Cindy looked back over her life, particularly these past eighteen sober years, she is certain that God never left her side; she is certain that every one of her experiences was necessary to prepare her to be the woman who is now able to intervene so gently into the lives of others, as Jane had entered into Cindy's.

Cindy is a gentle soul. In her traumatic, dramatic past she was also a gentle soul. She has the gift to help others develop their more gentle sides, too. That's the intent of her journey now. That's the mission she has devised for her center of healing. As she put it to me, "God and I are in joy." She wants to carry this message of hope and possibility and joy to every

man and woman who crosses her path, at her center and beyond its walls. She carried it to me. It has been my intent to
carry it now to you.

This is not the end of Cindy's story. With husband Roger
by her side, her concern for the well-being of others will
"sponsor" many of the necessary changes in all of those who
come her way so that they may discover what she finally
found *when it was her time to find it*.

CARRY THE MESSAGE

Let's look, for a moment, at the many "sponsors" in Cindy's
life. It's certain that many of her friends on the West Coast
tried to steer her in a different direction. Even though many
of them used drugs with her, a few were able to see that her
path was far more destructive than their own. Even though
they failed to get their message of concern across to Cindy, a
seed was planted. Every time someone attempted an intervention, she moved a little bit closer to the time she would
eventually heed God's call. This is simply how life works. The
unconscious is never fully *unconscious*. The words, the suggestions, and the dramatic as well as the quiet experiences are
filed away for future reference.

Cindy's mother acted as an important sponsor, too, when
she said at last, "Stay away." Cindy had never heard those
words before and they stuck with her. Although she didn't
doubt her mother's love, she understood that her mother
would not so foolishly give her a place to live ever again. This
knowledge made an impression on Cindy, but she managed
to bury it. Again, it was not yet her time to reverse her
course, but the information favoring the reversal was quickly
accumulating.

There were so many instances in Cindy's life that could

have helped her change directions. But they didn't. Or it might better be said, she didn't let them help her change directions. God was forever trying to get Cindy's attention. But her free will, her ego-run-riot, blocked out the words, the wisdom, the grace that was being offered. The wonderful realization that every one of us eventually comes to is that God will not go away. If he did, could we possibly be sharing this experience right now? I think not.

When Cindy entered her last treatment, was it because Jane, the woman who intervened at that juncture, offered some new information? Not likely. Cindy was simply ready to hear what had been said so many times before. What is terribly important to stress, however, is that had all of the other opportunities for changing direction not been offered to Cindy already, she might not have heeded the call that last time. It's not the first or the fiftieth attempt that creates the reversal. It's the right attempt. By this I mean, when the time is right, neither the words nor the specific message matters.

The "delivery person" doesn't matter either, because the message is God's. The uplifting truth is that one's Higher Power is in control. The alcoholic, the enabler, the intervener, the boss, the friend, the enemy—none of these is in control. We are all off the hook. That's the good news. But we are also bound to carry the message of our own hope and recovery to others wherever and whenever we can.

After getting sober, the next most important thing any one of us can do is to show others, by our own example, how different life can be. While it's certainly true that problems don't disappear just because we are sober, they are no longer more than we can handle. We can trust that the promises have not and will not mislead us. Allowing the newcomer to "see us in action" is the best education we can offer. It shows them that they, likewise, have the promises to look forward to. The real gift in this kind of sharing with the sponsee is that the sponsor is given another dose of recall regarding how true the promises actually are. The reminders are good for all of us. No one's program is beyond benefiting from reminders of how God works in our lives.

EIGHTEEN

FINAL THOUGHTS

No one is ever beyond the reach of God. No matter what a person's journey consists of, God has been present, often ignored, but present nonetheless. The sponsors who managed to get our attention, whether members of our fellowship or simply "on assignment" from God, are evidence of this. Glancing back at any one of the stories shared in this book will help to refresh your memory or dispel even the slightest remaining doubt that help was always available, though not always accepted, by every person who traveled this road. This will always be true—for you and me and for every other person alive.

When I began this series of interviews, I didn't doubt the impact other people had had on my own life. For years I have felt such gratitude for the role Pat played, specifically. I could see with little difficulty how my first husband, and now my second, have been key to my evolution. The many sponsors and friends who intervened all along the way have not gone unnoticed, at least in hindsight. But when I sat and listened to all of these men and women share their stories, I was profoundly moved to realize just how perfectly our lives do unfold! I was also forced to confront again the awareness that not everyone is saved. Some people who try to join our journey slip away. This will never be easily explained or understood. The mystery of why we didn't slip away is one of the miracles, but it suggests to me that since we didn't, we have a big job ahead of us.

When I was new in recovery, author Richard Bach gave me the hope and the inspiration I needed to continue getting up every morning and trusting that my life was purposeful when he included on the back cover of one of his books these words: "If you are reading this, your life's purpose hasn't yet been accomplished." We all have work to do. That's why we have been called to this moment in time.

Whatever you say to another person today at the grocery, in the department store, on the phone, at work, or in your own home might be the trigger that begins a new direction in that person's journey. Say what you will with love. Let's never forget that wherever we are, God is. Whatever words are coming from our heart are his to share. The message I love best and the one I choose to share as often as possible is the one the Dalai Lama gave at the conference I mentioned earlier: "Your job is to love one another. And if you can't do that, at least don't hurt one another."

Before closing, I want to summarize some key points about the role of sponsors and sponsees. First and foremost, both are extremely important to one another's peaceful journey. The founders of AA discovered firsthand and then kindly shared with us how necessary the union of two or more people was to the sobriety of any one person. The act of joining with another person on this journey through life is what lends meaning to our trip. It's through this *coming together* that we experience the hope and the wisdom that will make the destination worth reaching.

CARRY THE MESSAGE

Let's look at the sponsor's assignment first. Sponsors are the key to carrying the message. As sponsors we have a big responsibility. If we want the fellowship to thrive and offer to all of those alcoholics who come after us what we have found, we need to do our part in strengthening the message of hope, sharing the principles of the program, and being available to listen whenever someone reaches out to us for help.

There are some specifics that must be covered with a new sponsee. One of the first things we need to tell them is to avoid all of the places where alcohol is readily available, at least for the first few months. One of the first things my sponsor told me was that people seldom slip if they stay away from slippery places. The only sure way not to relapse is by not picking up a drink. If none are close at hand, it helps.

Another important direction for newcomers is to read a section from the Big Book, along with some other spiritual message, perhaps from a daily meditation book, every single day. This activity gives them a foundation for changing their current perspective on life and offers them a structure within which they can plan the rest of their day. Remember, most of us got here disheveled, disorganized, and distraught. Being told to do a simple task like reading a hopeful message every morning upon rising is an idea that is easily grasped and quickly relished, in fact. I can remember as though it were yesterday how relieved I felt over my first cup of coffee every morning that my life was under God's control. That's what the messages I read convinced me of and that's the only reason I felt the confidence to go on living one day at a time in the first year.

Attendance at meetings is a must, and sponsees need to be

guided to do this and to understand the importance of doing it. The best guidance comes from the sponsor's example. Good sponsors must live the program in the same way as they tell sponsees to live it. "Do as I do," in other words. Sponsees are guided to choose sponsors based on what they hear being said by them at meetings. The combination of good, consistent attendance at meetings and honest sharing about how the program is working in one's life is the substance of what a sponsee seeks when choosing a sponsor.

Explaining how the Steps are worked and have worked in the sponsor's life is extremely important, too. When I first read the Steps hanging on the wall at my first meeting, I was confused and a bit embarrassed by the thought of putting God in my life. I came into this fellowship much like all of the people who continue to come in. Past experience with church, strict clergymen, religious parents, or a punishing God doesn't make this part of our program attractive. When the Steps were explained to me, when their value was demonstrated and validated by my sponsor's experiences with them, I was more willing to study them and try to work them in my own life. Sponsees must understand the importance of doing this work as soon as possible. Telling them that AA's God loves them unconditionally does help.

REGULAR CONTACT

Sponsors need to insist that sponsees make daily contact with them or someone else in the program by phone, at coffee dates, or in fellowship meetings. Healing cannot occur in isolation. Every one of us reading this knows the tale of someone who disappeared from meetings and soon drank again. But there is an antidote that works 100 percent of the time. If every sponsor has at least one sponsee to talk to daily and every newcomer has at least one sponsor to talk to daily, no member of one of these dyads will wander away and get drunk again. The joining of two minds listening to both hearts makes recovery inevitable.

Emphasis on the Serenity Prayer, the Third Step prayer, and the many slogans is paramount, too. One of the most common failings when a newcomer comes to us is that he or she feels inadequate while tackling the various program "assignments." Reminding them that it's a process that will and should take the rest of their lives alleviates some of their concern about needing to do everything immediately. The slogans in particular help with this. "Keep it simple," "First things first," "One day at a time" can't be said too often or stressed too much to the newcomer.

While working all of the steps is mandatory, the Fourth and Fifth Steps, along with the Eighth and Ninth, must be done as soon as possible if the sponsee is going to get on track. Looking at who one has been, who one is now, and then contemplating who one wants to be in the future will offer the direction that has so often been missing from the "using life" of the confused newcomer. Stressing the impact that making amends to others will have on their day-to-day program just can't be done too often.

Sharing a personal example of how the Eighth and Ninth Steps worked for you will do a couple of very important things. It will allow sponsees to see your program at its best. It will serve as an example for them to follow. And it will remind you of the value of continuing to do this Step in your own life whenever you have behaved in an unfavorable way toward another person. Let's not forget that we never graduate. We are never done. As long as we are living we will need to correct our thinking, modify our behavior, and apologize for the transgressions that occurred before we chose to stop them. As sponsors, allowing our sponsees to see our failings, talking them over, and discussing with them what we should have done instead of what we did do, will enlighten them more than any other discussion could.

WORKS IN PROGRESS

We are not saints. We are works in progress. That's what is so valuable about the sponsor-sponsee relationship. No one stands still in this exchange of information. The teacher keeps learning in the very act of sharing while the student is learning, too. As I have said before, the sponsor needs the sponsee just as much as the sponsee needs the sponsor. Some days I think even more!

Now let's turn to the sponsees for a moment. Reviewing their "assignment" is just as important as reviewing the assignment of the sponsor. Sponsees need to make it understood that they are intent on living a new kind of life. They can best do this by reaching out, preferably on a daily basis, to their sponsor or some other person they have made a good connection with at a meeting. They need to consistently attend meetings. They need to willingly ask questions, read program literature, and do all of the Steps completely as often as necessary. They need to make a commitment to daily prayer and meditation. Avoiding isolation is a must, too. In isolation, relying only on the information any one person carries around in his head, is a sure way to remain in the throes of the disease.

Sponsees simply must become accountable for all of their actions. They must willingly take responsibility for all past actions, too, particularly those times when problem behavior was the catalyst for a fiasco. Sponsees have the opportunity to make right whatever their wrongs were in the past. Not taking advantage of this opportunity might suggest to the rest of us that the sponsee isn't really ready to go to any lengths to find what we have found. But staying in our lives, continuing to go to meetings, continuing to read what we have suggested, and continuing to make the calls that are necessary in order to stay sober and enhance the healing process will improve the sponsees' chances of eventually finding the sobriety that Bill W. and Dr. Bob and the rest of us have found.

Every one of us will find his or her own unique way to live and share the messages of this program. There is not a particular way anything has to be done. There are very few things that have to be explicitly stressed by each one of us, either, other than the often repeated "Don't drink, go to meetings, and read the Big Book." If every sponsee did only these three things, not a single one of them would ever end up back on the streets.

I want to stress once again the importance of all of the "other sponsors" in our lives. We could not have gotten here and stayed here if a number of other significant people had not crossed our paths along the way. I don't want to ever suggest that the only people who count are the ones who share our program. They are absolutely necessary, of course, to our sobriety, but we must share the accolades for our recovery with many other people as well. The *teachers* were always present. And even when we were at our worst, we were learning something; even when we didn't realize a message was getting through, it was. That's the marvel of the human condition. Nothing goes unregistered in our mind, and it patiently waits there for us to notice it. We will learn what we need to learn, sometime, someplace, in some way. Likewise, as long as we are showing up in the lives of others, we will be helping others to learn. That's the way God intended it. It's his will and our life's work.

I cherish the reality that there are no accidents. I love the awareness that you and I are constantly "on assignment." I still remember hearing one of my sponsors say that her favorite prayer was "Send me in, God. I am ready!" At the time I wasn't sure I could agree. Where might I be sent? Now I know. Now I rejoice that where I was sent was here with you. Thanks for coming to the party.

TWELVE STEPS OF
ALCOHOLICS ANONYMOUS*

1. We admitted we were powerless over alcohol—that our lives had become unmanageable.
2. Came to believe that a Power greater than ourselves could restore us to sanity.
3. Made a decision to turn our will and our lives over to the care of God *as we understood Him.*
4. Made a searching and fearless moral inventory of ourselves.
5. Admitted to God, to ourselves, and to another human being the exact nature of our wrongs.
6. Were entirely ready to have God remove all these defects of character.
7. Humbly asked Him to remove our shortcomings.
8. Made a list of all persons we had harmed, and became willing to make amends to them all.
9. Made direct amends to such people wherever possible, except when to do so would injure them or others.
10. Continued to take personal inventory and when we were wrong promptly admitted it.
11. Sought through prayer and meditation to improve our conscious contact with God *as we understood Him,* praying only for knowledge of His will for us and the power to carry that out.
12. Having had a spiritual awakening as the result of these steps, we tried to carry this message to alcoholics, and to practice these principles in all our affairs.

---

* The Twelve Steps of AA are taken from *Alcoholics Anonymous,* 3d ed., published by AA World Services, Inc., New York, N.Y., 59–60. Reprinted with permission of AA World Services, Inc. (See editor's note on copyright page.)

ABOUT THE AUTHOR

Karen Casey is the best-selling author of *Each Day a New Beginning, Daily Meditations for Practicing the Course, Keepers of the Wisdom,* and numerous other books. She has also written two new books for girls: *Girls Only!* and *Girl to Girl.* Her signature book, *Each Day a New Beginning,* has sold three million copies. Karen enjoys golfing and riding her Harley with her husband. She lives in Minneapolis, Minnesota, and Naples, Florida.